Laughter
that Will Lift Your Spirits

by Paul W. Tastad

DORRANCE
PUBLISHING CO
EST. 1920
PITTSBURGH, PENNSYLVANIA 15238

Dorrance Publishing Co
585 Alpha Drive
Suite 103
Pittsburgh, PA 15238
Visit our website at *www.dorrancebookstore.com*

ISBN: 978-1-4809-4688-0
eISBN: 978-1-4809-4665-1

Advice/Sayings

Good advice "Don't fall apart, but try and stay in one piece."

Advice from a photographer Stay in the picture. Be in focus.

Don't wait to be alarmed when you wake up.

In a small town you don't want to be the talk of the town.

Don't wave to your friend at an auction unless you want to buy something.

If you want help you just have to say "the word."

The librarian has good advice. She says no matter how much you are attracted to the cover of a book, until you read it or get to know it better you never know what is between the covers.

If you can't win practice losing gracefully.

When we lost it, it bothers others. our temper

When you are wound up it is going to take awhile to unwind.

Advice from a bee keeper If the deal is to sweet you may want to back away from it.

The number one place we want someone to autograph is a check made out to us.

Advice from a electrician Don't be left out in the dark.

The number in life we all want is the winning number.

A poultry farmer says don't put all your eggs in one basket.

Who wants to know things? Inquiring minds

An astronaut was the first to say "He took off like a rocket."
He was also the first to say "Prices are skyrocketing."

When we are standing in line what we all want to hear. "Next"

A bee farmer that feels overwhelmed we say he is bedazzled.

As we get older our bodies shrink. That is called "downsizing."

Advice from a trucker. Never stay too long in any one place. When you leave don't look back. It will keep you from going on and you may have an accident.

The sanitation worker says don't rush or be in a hurry. Remember "Haste makes waste."

A true shopper who loves to spend money says her time is well spent.

The clock maker says that many things don't work out for people because their timing is off.

The builder says most people in life want to start on the ground floor.

When the weather man's mother got really upset it was the Mother of all storms.

It is better to be a half wit than have no wit at all.

A hunter says be careful when you shot because there will be a time when you are down to your last shot.

A pilot said if you don't learn to fly right you are going to end having some rough landings.

It is difficult to go forward in life if you always have to watch your back.

Most grandparents operate on a stand bye basis. They are to be ready only when needed.

A runner says you need to see how things will look in the long run. At times you need to be willing to go the distance.

A corn farmer was the first to have his jokes called corny.

A dairy farmer said we need to remember rain or sunshine the cows still need to be milked. He also said don't milk the cow dry because than you will lose your cash cow.

Advice from a laundry worker Be careful not to get any stains in your life because they may not come to in the wash.

Advice from a plumber There are some things you just need to flush down the toilet and forget about them.

How many people make a crowd? three What is the number we all take care of the most? One because we are number one. What is a high number and a happy number? A high five

Advice from a skydiver He says if you are going to jump try to keep both feet on the ground.

A deep thinker can get lost anywhere. He is usually lost in thought.

What line most people dread the most deadline

What most people have trouble doing is connecting the dots.

Who says "It is not my fault?" Practically everyone

Advice from a cleaner
If there is food leftover polish it off.
Don't give in to feelings but just suck it up.
If there is too much dust in the room it makes you wonder if someone has
recently died. You know from dust to dust we return.

Who says "Thank your lucky stars?" Astronomer

The only thing people want to share is the blame.

Facts that haven't been used for awhile become cold facts.

Most people want foresight to see what lies ahead instead of hindsight when
they see what is in back of them.

Who says "I tripped him up?" A local travel agent.

When a pirate is cold they say "shiver my timbers."

Stroke of luck is when a golfer gets a hole in one.

Someone in the past who was hip, was called a hippy.

In life if you want to look busy or important hold a phone in your ear. Also
you may point to the phone and say and put a finger to your mouth that means
they have to hush it up.

A welder says life can be riveting if we let it.

A man said he rarely started any projects. His Dad always said don't start something if you are not prepared to finish it.

A shoe salesman is famous for the saying "If the shoe fits wear it."

Why do we count down, but don't count up?

Don't crow about your own achievements.

When your feet are killing you, you may need to start wearing the right shoe size.

Good advice from the weatherman is that this too will blow over.

The only thinking a lot of people do is wishful thinking.

You will never get anywhere in life if you only break even.

A cowgirl gives advice. When you finally break one guy in, it is best to stay with him. It can be difficult to start breaking someone else in.

When you smile all the time people wonder what you are up to.

He didn't just have a smile.. He wore a know it all smile.

How can you make a pretty mess?

When it comes to the scale we all have a tipping point.

Good advice from a landscaper. Don't plant your feet in someone else's yard.

Why do we use the term common sense? Everyone knows it isn't common anymore.

Procrastinators are getting worse. Now instead of saying they will do it tomorrow, they say they will do it the day after tomorrow.

Truckers are bad at procrastinating they say they will do it down the road and after a few more miles.

A trucker tells a someone who is worried about something in the future, he says we will cross that bridge when we come to it.

Unless they are choking you really don't want to tell someone to spit it out.

When people are afraid they are always ready to stand behind you.

A hunter says he doesn't have goals but has targets instead. He says nobody is perfect and everyone's aim is off once in awhile. Just make sure to set your sites on what you want in life.

Advice from a forest ranger is that we all have to follow our own paths in life.

Advice from a bee keeper   Bee all that you can bee. Everyone deserves to have a little honey in their lives.

We want a cereal with a snappy comeback.

Whether we are black or white we all worry about going grey.

We no longer say it is the best that money can buy. We know now days everyone uses credit cards.

Money may not bring you happiness but for most people it sure can put a smile on their face.

In relationships couples need to follow the yellow light principle and proceed with caution.

Most adults don't like games. They say don't be playing games with me.

I am sure there will be pie in heaven. Haven't you heard about pie in the sky?

If there are deep thinkers than there has to be shallow thinkers.

Don't you hate it when you are ready to blame someone and they say don't blame me.

Everyone but the one surprised loves surprise parties.

Nobody wants to be owed a debt of gratitude when you can be owed a debt of money.

Many people with titles think they are entitled to more.

The turn you want to make is a turn for the better.

A miner suggests that sometimes when we don't find the success we want in life we have to learn to dig a little deeper.

A beauty contestant may have a winsome smile but without talent she may never win.

I don't worry I just get over anxious.

If you could sell it lots of people would line up to buy it. It is time.

Some people are not really good they are only marginally good.

People aren't born losers. They have to work at getting that way.

If pushed far enough we all have a breaking point.

Most people like to volunteer that is volunteer someone else.

A trucker says sometimes to work things out you just need to go on down the road.

Lawyers tell their clients to say this "nothing."

Baseball player says to watch out for those curves thrown at us.

We want people to say it isn't so.

When your looking for surprises you might want to buy some cracker jacks.

In the country there were so many snakes. I can just hear Grandma saying "Land snakes alive."

In a running race you come in second. Should't you be called the runner up?

Even worms need their grub.

It is hard when you rush to get somewhere and than get there and wonder what you were in a rush to get there for.

Yesterday's new is called history.

If there is an after thought is there a before thought?

A railroad engineer said that even the best of plans can be derailed.

Only a linesman really knows what a hotline is.

Bug people like to say about babies that they are as cute as a bug.

There are people who work hard and those who are hardly working.

Go to echo canyon if you like to hear the sound of your voice.

Firemen's children love the game chute and ladders.

A miner says you may not want to sit on a powder keg.

Who was the first person to say "ho ho ho?" It was a local gardner.

Who said "Do you feel the heat?" A furnace repair man

A forest ranger gave good advice. He said if you are in the woods and a bear stands on his two legs and comes towards you. What you need to do is give the bear a bear hug. The bear is badly in need of a hug.

Who first said "It's your move." A moving company said that to their customers.

Someone who drinks too much coffee gets perky.

When a fireman quits he gives his burn notice.

Who said "Let me straighten this out." A perfectionist who saw a picture hanging crooked.

You can wear anything you like but this on your birthday. Your birthday suit.

Who is looking for a free ride? a hitch hiker

You don't want your investment counselor to lose your trust.

The advice of a parking attendant is we need to know when to park it.

When you dream in the daytime it is a day dream.

When they sell dirt it is pay dirt.

A furnace man sometimes has to vent his anger.

When someone says you are in ship shape you have to wonder. Do you really want to be in the shape of a ship?

A cat with a bad disposition is called a sour puss.

If you stay quiet during a discussion people will think you know something. They won't know you were just daydreaming.

A stubborn pig farmer is said to be pig headed.

Whoever said the pen is mightier than the sword has not fought a battle with a pen.

The trap you don't want to get caught in is a speed trap.

The bread man said some people don't even know what side to butter the bread on. This could lead to a long discussion.

Getting old is like good wine. The older it gets the better it is.

A cleaner says she always has a bucketful of things to do.

Who says "I have got you on my mind?" A mind reader of course.

What you did may not be insane, but it definitely borders on insanity.

When you ask a beggar to work they often beg off.

A man tells the railroad engineer not to railroad him into another job.

I am a marked man. I have tattoos all over me.

It is good there is a window of opportunity because the door for many is closed.

When someone says they have nothing to lose it usually means they have already lost everything by gambling earlier.

Don't be like the leafs and turn on me.

Life is full of ups and downs says the elevator lady.

You want time to slow down attend a piano recital.

Adults can act like mountains when they blow their top.

A story is too long if by the time you get to the end nobody can remember the beginning.

When someone is having a Mars attack. Quick give them a mars candy bar.

I was on top of my game. Another guy said get off it. We want to play too.

Advice from a race car driver. He says always keep your engine running because you never know what you are going to need to take off.

Some people are not good at tracing. They have to retrace their steps.

When you sleep with the bedbugs how do you keep them from biting you?

It is hard to be a guide when you are accused of misguiding people.

When you work at a cemetery you don't want to feel a spirit moving.

Most of the time if the job is easy they won't ask you to do it.

When chickens fly over a fire they get hot wings.

When you can use the science you learn it is called applied science.

When a rock star is depressed we say he has reached rock bottom.

You may be right but you are not sure. The other person is sure they are right. Sometimes you need to yield to the right of way.

Sleeping on the floor of a ship is definitely a hardship.

When someone says can I give you advice. The main response is only if I ask for it.

Advice from an English teacher
Ask the right questions,
Know when to pause and put a comma in your life.
Live life with lots of action verbs.
Know when to stop period.

A seamstress when upset says "oh darn." When she has been sick and starts to get better we say she is on the mend.

The term we get from India is "Holy Cow."

A watchmaker hates it when people say they are just killing time.

A gambler with a problem is always saying you betcha.

Who first said "A mind is a terrible thing to waste?" Your local sanitation worker.

Who said "There is beauty in ashes?" A fireman from fire house number 9.

Who said if you want to see growth and things change you have to be willing to get down and get dirty? A local landscaper.

A golfer likes others to be happy and play. He tells them they can play through.

A grower says there are too many empty headed people around who let others plants idea in their heads.

A skydiver said he was the original fall guy. He said when you jump you may want to land with both feet on the ground.

A photographer said may many people fail in life because they don't really see the big picture.

A gambler said we would get more in life if we only played our cards right.

When a cleaner thinks your right he says "spot on." Cleaners like to tell clean jokes.

Give someone an inch and they think their a ruler.

A dairy farmer said when he greet people we should learn to say "cheese." It makes them think of taking a picture when they smile.

Never second guess what you first said or you will be disappointed with what you said.

Who says "I don't mind?" Many disobedient children.

If you are feeling hot you want to think cold thoughts.

What we need to learn from card players. We need not to overplay our hands. We need to know when to have a poker face. We need to know when to fold. We need to know when to call a bluff. We need to know the importance of playing a straight.

When a weather man talks too much we say he is long winded.

Just remember if you finish last in race that nice guys finish last.

Who said "There is something rotten in Denmark?" It was either a jealous Swede or someone who visited a pig farm in Denmark.

A stockbroker says when something sells well it is a hot commodity.

A hole digger says lots of time people with their talk and actions dig themselves into a hole. If the hole is too deep they may have a problem getting themselves out of it.

In Italy if they are upset with you they simply give you the boot.

A trucker coming to the end of his life says "This is the end of the road for me. I see my exit is coming up."

Astronomers always want to be the center of their universe.

"If you can't stand the heat stay out of the kitchen." Many thought that meet when someone was cooking. A fireman explained that was true. It really had to do with fires in the kitchen. One man said it is the same to him because when his wife cooks there usually is a fire.

A crowd usually means that there is no elbow room. Everyone is rubbing elbow with each other.

When you say you want a surprise you may want to clarify what kind of surprise you want. There are good surprises and than quite a few that aren't so good.

What most people don't want to be left with is the bill.

In life are we ever more than half listening?

We say "When I am good, I am very very good. I want people to know that I am good and I want to be awarded for being good. When I am bad very bad I look for someone to blame for my behavior."

What do you call a boy with bad breath? A lonely boy.

What is the point most of us don't want to reach? breaking point.

Tarzan says "When in Africa lots of people get the jungle fever.

An eye doctor said you need to go into a relationship with your eyes wide open. You also need to be able to see long distance to see where this relationship is going.

The eye doctor says the fastest thing is a blink.

I thought I was wrong, but than I realized I wasn't. I just thought I made a mistake.

What everyone wants us to sign on. The dotted line.

A sign at a loan company said "Money can't buy happiness but it sure can buy a lot of other things."

How can you hang on and hang loose at the same time?

When you are at a loss for words, you could really use a dictionary.

It it was a perfect world than you wouldn't be in it.

The watchmaker says at the end of the day that things are winding down.

There are deep thinkers, shallow thinkers, fuzzy thinkers and older people with lots of their mind if they could just remember what it is.

Careers

The company was innovative and said they were full of ideas. They let one employee go. When he was asked why they fired him, he said he had no idea.

Swimmer in business
He knew he was over his head.
His business was under water.
He was drowning in debt.
He was overcome with a flood of emotions.
He had a pool of office workers depending on him.
He needed a loan to stay afloat.
He finally found a friend in a loan office who gave him a loan.
He called him his life savior.

The clock family all worked in the clock factory.
Grandfather clock was the oldest.
Several were cuckoo clocks, but every family has some of them.
There was an alarm clock always upset by something.
The most dangerous was the ticking time bomb ready to go off.
There was the lazy one with time on his hands.
There was the one who always watched the clock.
One said "You never know when your time is up".
The nagger says "I have told you this time after time".
Some we don't know how they will work out, only time will tell.
Some give timely advice.
We must remember time marches on and doesn't stand still for anyone.

Sweet shop
Where you go if you have a sweet tooth.
Candy and Sugar run the store.

A lot of sweet talk goes on there.
They call everyone sweetie or honey.
They have a lot of sweet deals.
They definitely know how to sweeten the pot.

A former seamstress now works as a psychologist. She looks into the pattern of behavior of her clients.

A man said he worked too long at an amusement park. He was in charge of the merry-go-round. He said now he has trouble because his ideas and thoughts just keep going around and around.

A man said he worked with a lot of dummies. I said that isn't nice to call your coworkers that. He said he works with test dummies in car crashes.

The highlight for people who work with lights is when they go to the festival of lights.

A vampire was working evenings. We may say he was moonlighting.

She has been working in the lighting store for so long she is considered a real fixture.

A pilot said he just couldn't learn to relax on his down time.

An engineer has a one track mind.

A sign for a hair dresser said "Let us mess with your hair."

A sign for a wedding planner said "We help you with all the planning for the wedding. All you need to do is find a groom."

Sign at an airport says "We will take you above and beyond."

A newspaper reporter is in trouble when he has nothing to report.

When there are too many bosses at the top of a company we say the company is top heavy.

A sign at a clothing store said "You may be a pauper but we will help you dress like a king."

The gardener's helper asked him if they were close to done. He said we haven't even broken ground yet.

A young man said one summer he helped his Grandfather in his clock shop where they fixed clocks. Many times they had to work around the clock.

The only one who wants to see more problems is a psychologist.

I took back books to the half price book store. After looking them over the clerk said he would take the paperbacks but didn't want the hardcovers. I said put them on a sale table and say half price on it and I am sure they will sell.

It was at a can factory where workers came up with the idea of going to the can when they had to use the bathroom. The dance the "Can Can" was started at the can factor. The manager is very canny. He always says "Can I be candid with you?"

Lawn workers sometimes do all right. One said he was raking in the money.

When hiring new workers at a grocery store they look at their marketing skills.

What every salesman wants his customers to be sold on is the idea.

The post office is working with the sanitation department to bring us junk mail.

An orchard grower says some people are like fruit even with their best efforts they don't produce any fruit.

A worker at the steel plant was so upset that the manger said he was bent out of shape. The band at the plant of course uses steel drums.

I love my new job. I get to lay down on the job. I test mattress.

A dishwasher says he has to scrape to get by.
He was told to wash up.
He wanted things to sparkle
He wanted to work with silver.
He warns people about hot plates.
He says that he can see through glasses.
Before he goes out he likes to rinse off.
He wanted to get to the bottom of the pan so he could see himself.
He would like to be in a scrub free zone.
The dishwasher was taught to take whatever was dished out.

Life for a coffee shop owner is often a daily grind.

I worked for the phone company so long I began to think of Ma Bell as a second Mother.

The water was tested by the water department. The one worker said there is lead in the water. The other worker said well get the lead out. The water worker feels the water pressure.

The lifeguard said his job wasn't all that easy. There was jealousy and competition and an undercurrent of uneasiness.

The ad said I would be working with windows and have a chance to get high up the ladder. I thought great a job working with computers. I could handle that easy. It turns out I wash windows on a high ladder.

At the company they announced that all the nonessential workers could go home at noon. Later the manger saw the boss and said "I guess we are all that is essential."

It helps miners in their work if they have tunnel vision.

One guy who worked in the fruit department was called "Peaches." He always wore a little peach fuzz.

A jeweler always wants to talk about the chain of events of the day. He had to let one worker go for being a weak link in the store.

At the water department that sent out a letter telling people they needed to conserve on their water use. Unfortunately the letter was so watered down.

The pilot was happy when his career got off the ground.

A smart barber is said to be razor sharp.

The postal worker was hugging a box. When asked why he said "The box said handle with care."

Carpenter to helper "Put away that silly putty and get to work."

The politician had a wife that was mean, talked too much and actually no one could stand her. He always took her with him when he campaigned. He was after the sympathy vote.

A guy says he just lost his park job. He was in the park to work and two of his friends stopped by to visit and before you know it, he lost track of time. I asked what his job was. He said to put the signs "Wet Paint" on park benches.

A trail guide was taking a group on a hike. One of the people on the hike was continually asking questions and annoying others. The guide suggested he take some back country trails. The man asked "What if I get lost?" The guide thought we can only hope.

His Dad is a landscaper. When he gives him jobs to do and than leaves the boy aways puts on his jeans with the grass stains to prove he was working.

A druggist said not until he retied did he feel drug free.

It can be rough being a stunt man. When he does certain stunts the producer says "You pull that stunt once more and you are out of here".

At the cemetery they have a cemetery walk every year. Of course, the caretaker makes sure they all get rakes to use on their walk.

She works with small problems. She is a child psychologist.

When two power companies merge they say more power to you.

A cleaner says you don't just sweep you make a clean sweep.

A guard in trouble is said to be off guard.

It is hard to be in a competitive business and to mind your own business.

A used car place is run by the Lemmon brothers.

I asked the clown how he got to be a clown. He said it started in elementary school when he was the class clown.

A cement worker to another cement worker says I don't like that last crack you made.

A man owed two gas stations on either side of the state line. On the front of both stations it said "Last Chance" and on the back of the sign it said "Not a Chance."

Digging holes can be a boring job. A man said there is not a hole lot going on here.

It is hard for a trapper when he doesn't have a good tracking record.

The comedian took his act to the state prison. He was asked not to come back. They said he was a riot.

A loyal worker was asked what planet he was from. He said Planet Ford.

A sign at a company says we will help you plan for your future. We can help you make secure plans. While waiting inside to talk to someone, I over heard one employee ask another what she was doing that night. She said I don't know I don't have any plans.

Only the masonry guy can get by telling his workers to go lay a brick.

Some salesmen have a hard time selling. They find it is often a hard sell.

The baker worked all the time with weights and measurements. He was the one who came up with the name of a cake called the pound cake.

The mail carrier stalls when she says she will be there as soon as everything is sorted out.

A builder says we can build the structure, but it takes the couple to make it a home.

A model to a fashion designer says she needs more coverage.

Fortune tellers are starting to work with the weatherman so they can get better predictions.

When the post office workers are against something they organize a stamping out party.

Definitely Tom is not a daily planner. Come to think of it, he is not a planner at all. Only thing you can say about him is don't plan on him.

Boss to parking attendant at a hotel says you are going to have to go if you don't quit playing bumper cars.

The tobacco salesman didn't come into work. He wasn't feeling up to snuff.

The party house had a motto that said "party on." They have been getting a lot of business when they started to offer pity parties.

My cousin has a dead end job. He works at the cemetery

Dairy farmers are smart they know the difference between butter and margarine.

When a weather man is upset he says someone is stealing his thunder.

An important job in the watch factory is the man who reads the minutes.

A worker who writes for a tabloid magazine said he couldn't find the dirt on someone. He was told to dig a little deeper.

At their job the employees must sign statement that they promise never to tell the employers secret. It the secret gets out the business could be ruined. They work at Victoria Secrets.

The new pickup service at the grocery store is not working out well. One girl said she stood there for over an hour and no one picked her up.

What we would all like to tell the IRS is to mind their own business.

A trucker said too many close calls can leave you feeling like a wreck.

The man worked under cover in a bedding store.

Someone asked a shoplifter how she was doing. She says things are picking up.

When a sanitation worker takes a trip it is called a junket.

Our banks need to take us into account.

I asked the nun how she liked being a nun.   She said it is an acquired habit. One nun didn't like it all. For her it was a bad habit.

A daycare worker says most of his work is child' play.

A daycare worker says you lead by example. When he tells the children to take a nap, he takes one also.

Doctors and Mental Health

A doctor tells his patient to take a deep breath and then let it out again. The patient says he can't because he ran out of breath awhile ago.

A chiropractor said he wanted to be known as Mr. Soft Touch.

When a doctor marries a corn farmer what can you say but "Ah shucks."

A cleaning lady married the doctor she cleaned for. He was a surgeon. When she found out how he went into surgery she said things are going to have to change. She made him scrub real good before surgery. This is where we get the term scrub doctor.

A patient at a mental hospital drew people upside down. He says he feel his world is upside down.
Another drew half a man. When asked why he said he is not all there.

A heart doctor said it is terrible. People keep bring patients to him in hope that they he can find that they have a heart.

While touring the mental hospital I noticed a room full of baskets and one man working on them. I was told he was a basket case.

You don't say to someone at a metal hospital. Are you out of your mind?

What is the name of a lazy doctor? Dr. Do Little

A lady told the psychologist that she wanted to bare her soul to him. He said that won't be necessary. He said let's just peel off one layer at a time. I want to leave something for my imagination.

What a doctor should never say "So I made a little mistake what are you going to do sue me?"

My dad thought he was a psychologist. He was always giving us advice and telling us what we should to. I thought of him as a pop psychologist.

A sign on a foot doctor's office "Remember Feet First."

A nurse who works in surgery had to help take out a diseased liver. That night she went home asked her mother what they having for dinner. Her mother said liver.

The bone doctor was showing off his bone collection to a friend. The neighbor came over and brought his big hunting dog. The dog thought he was in dog heaven. The dog took after those bones and growled if anybody came near him. Needless to say the doctor and neighbor are not on the best terms.

A nurse says be good to me I am the one hooking you up.

A man was getting his ears checked. He said he was going to a hearing. The ear doctor was the first one to say "Lend me your ear."

Two doctors are looking over the symptoms of a patient. The one asks the other doctor what he thinks. He says your guess is as mine.

It is hard to be a nurse and still be carefree.

The only doctor that knows know the inside of you is the doctor of internal medicine.

The only reason a vampire is sick is because they got hold of some bad blood.

I work at the hospital. The food in the cafeteria is so bad that I make sure I eat there every day. So far I have lost ten pounds.

The real reason doctor and uses wear gloves during surgery is because they don't want your blood on their hands.

You may not want to go to a small hospital for an operation. I hear they are operating on a small budget.

If you don't like the way your doctor operators you can ask for another one.

Two nurses were talking outside a patient's room where the door was partly open and he was able to hear what they were saying. One said "Dr. Olson is so excited about the operation. It will be his first time doing this surgery. "Yes" the other one said "I heard he has been reading books about this type of surgery. Well let's just hope he gets it right." Later the doctor came back to check on the patient only to find that he had disappeared.

You may want this one doctor. I hear he is a smooth operator.

An eye doctor said before he makes decisions he likes to get in the right frame of mind. The eye doctor says when you learn something new it can be a real eye opener.

A woman said her husband is so lazy. She took him to the eye doctor, because he had a lazy eye.

A doctor says that they say laughter is the best medicine. He decided to try it and tell patents funny stories about the mistakes that doctors make. Instead of laughing they would get a panicked look on their face and want to cancel their next appointment.

A psychologist is listening to a patient. The patient says he makes promises to his wife that he can't keep. He covers up what he does at work. And even when caught he can't admit he does anything wrong. The psychologist asked if he every thought about running for a political office.

At a mental hospital a patient held onto a book like it was the wheel of a car, and had a panicked look on his face. When asked what was wrong with him, they said he had taught driver's ed for over twenty years.

The doctor asked the patient where he hurt. He pointed to his pocketbook.

When a swimmer is having mental problems he goes off the deep end.

At the mental hospital an announcement came over the loud speaker. Would you please quit play the song "Crazy."

A section of a mental hospital has the patients that are the most depressed. When I went there one of them asked if I was down with them.

The former head of a mental hospital said he felt like a squirrel. We are both storing the nuts in one place.

An upset nurse had been giving shots. She said she was so upset she couldn't even shoot straight.

Patient to nurse please no more shots. I am already all shot up.

Man at mental hospital asked to get his hearing tested. The doctor asked what was wrong. He said for three years he had been hearing voices. Now for the past month he hasn't heard them.

When we have pain it is the doctor's gain.

My son can't have a simple fracture he has to have a compound fracture.

I meet the nurse who hold the shot record in the hospital.
She likes to look over the area where she shot people and examine her needle-work.

It says there is a large nursing staff working at the hospital. I hope they get help with their weight problem.

What the cleaner wants the doctor to give her a clean bill of health.

After surgery a nurse says she has seen more of the working on Jack's insides than she cared to.

The doctor told the man's wife that he suffered a hair line fracture. She said not my husband because he is bald.

The eye doctor says before you sign a deal look in their eyes to see if they have shifty eyes.

When a pig farmer is sick they say he has the swine flu.

Nobody but a bone doctor would call bones lovely bones.

At the hospital the doctors could not figure out what to do about a serious problem. They said we need to call in an expert. Later in the day one doctor asked the other doctor if that wasn't his mother sitting out in the waiting room. He said yes, you said you need to call in an expert and nobody is more an expert than she is.

Who tells the actors before they go on stage to break a leg? It was traced back to a bone doctor.

A man went to the eye doctor. He said there was something wrong with his blinker.

At the hospital a salesman was complaining about all the samples he had to hand out. A lab worker said don't complain. I work with urine samples.

His jokes were so sick the only place he was allowed to tell them was in the hospital.

A sick dairy farmer says his stomach is churning.

The couple was getting on in years. The husband was in the hospital for surgery. His wife was in the room with him when the surgery was over. Her friend Edith came to visit. She looked at the man who was sleeping and said "Oh my doesn't he look just awful?" The wife said "Edith he has looked that way for the past forty years. They can't change his looks but can help him get well."

A bone doctor says he loves break dancing. He get a lot of business from people who do it.

Announcement over the loud speaker at a mental hospital said there are snacks of fruit, nuts and crackers in the lounge.

A girl jumped off of a three story building. The press was interviewing the doctor who worked with her. The doctor said it is amazing that she has no broken bones. That is almost unheard of. A reporter asked how she is doing. He said oh she died an hour ago.

If you listen to much to a doctor you become indoctrinated.

At the mental hospital the patent said "I don't know why I am here. They say it is a crazy world out there and the way I see it I fit right in."

The dentist asked the patient what he thought about something. The patient said he was numb.

In the doctor's oath it says how they promise to treat you to the best of their ability and not to admit to making any mistakes.

When they say "It is a little crazy around here" they could be talking about a mental hospital or they could mean working in a school.

A foot doctor said that he and his son were not close. He said his son was at least thirty feet apart from him

When someone is sick sometimes we say they caught the fever.

An older man had his checkup with a lady doctor. When the doctor was done she said "I couldn't find anything wrong with you". He said I should have married you. My wife has a whole list of what is wrong with me.

A runner complains to the doctor that he feels tired and run down. The doctor says you need to stop your running around.

The man had an extra large nose that was crooked in the middle. He had a sore throat for a long time. He decided to have it checked. He went to the ear nose and throat doctor.
When the doctor came into the room he looked at him and said "Whoa what a hooker. You are going to have to have plastic surgery or at least see a specialist if you want help with that."

At the eye doctor one of the workers was a young Hispanic worker. The eye doctor says to him "I know this is an eye doctor place but every time someone says something to you quit saying "Si"

The young man at the eye doctor said he had trouble because every time he was at a party and saw a pretty girl he winked. He said the boyfriends didn't like it and were giving him black eyes.

The doctor complained about his wife's family. She has a large family and they have lots of kids. They come over almost every night and start coughing and sneezing. Than they ask "Is there a doctor in the house?"

A man was having surgery the next day. He was in the hospital. Two nurses were talking. One said you know Dr. Heinz is not a morning person. The other said she knows he has even said he is fuzzy thinking in the morning. The other one said I know he forgets things in the morning. The nurse said I am afraid one of these days he is going to make a mistake. Turning to the patient she asked when is your surgery? He whispered seven in the morning.

The eye doctor was having me read the letters. I said I don't feel comfortable reading your letters.

We all want to be first except if it comes to an operation. We never want to be the first for the doctor.

The doctor asked the patient if he had ever had the pain before. He said yes seven years ago. What does it mean? It means that its back.

Two older guys who hadn't seen each other for awhile were visiting. One told the other one that he had been seeing quite a bit of his doctor. The other one asked him if he had been sick. No just playing golf

Family

A little boy said to his mother "I want a bracelet just like my Uncle Joe. You know the one he wears on his ankle.

When his cousin played the part of a fool in a play he didn't have to act.

An undertaker talking to his kids. I don't appreciate your playing dead.

It is hard to be the teenage son of a pilot. He has to get clearance before he can take off.

My dad wants to eat all the time. Overtime I ask him something he says let me chew on it.

A hunter when he took his middle school children to the mall or on trips he would give them a time when they were to meet him. He would tell them to sure and be there, he didn't want to have to hunt them down.

A boy's brother is one year older. The boy does everything his brother does and follows him everywhere. You know what his nickname is? Shadow

A boy about to become a teenager asked his Mom if he was going to be able to kiss any girl when you told him not to give her any lip. She answered you know when you tell a secret you say it is from my lips to yours. Do that and you will be okay.

Your Grandmother was fat and not very pretty. Your Aunt comes to see you. You haven't seen her in a number of years. She says you are the spitting image of your Grandmother. Life can be so unfair.

When a Chinese man hurries his children along he says "chop, chop."

A girl left the hog farm she was raised on in Iowa. She loved her Dad and the farm and would do something to keep it in her memory. She wore her hair in pigtails.

My twelve year old son came home with some of his friends. I asked what was up. He said they had been talking and they wanted to know what an idiot looked like, so I thought I would show them Jeff my older brother.

Our grandfather was so much fun. When we were young he would take us places. We went to a crowded restaurant where the parking lot was almost full. He told us to go inside and get a table while he would find a parking place. Later he came in and said "Those fool bikers parking their bikes all in row. I back into one bike and they all tip over". You never saw bikers move faster running out to see what happened to their bikes.

A girl asked her brother how he liked the cookies she made. He said they were crummy.

His father worked for the railroad. To remember him he has spiked hair.

My nephew is not welcomed to go with the hunter anymore. When he was with them and got impatient he would say "Well shoot anyway."

A lady said she felt like she was a mother hen.
When her chicks grew up they left the coop.
Now when they have gotten older they have come back to roost.

A boy had a dog named Spot. Unfortunately his mother was cleaner and was always looking for a spot removal.

A banker's son says something cute and the banker says he is going to coin that phrase.

Her son was such a good reader he could read between the lines.

A man said he got to be a runner, because when he was little he would talk to his Mother and she would say "Now run along."

Some guys were giving one guy a bad time. He said "My Mom didn't raise no fool." His friend said "Didn't you tell me that your Dad raised you?"

Our Dad tells us things he wants us to remember. Later he gives us Pop quizzes on what he has told us.

My Uncle believes in the saying "If at first you don't succeed try, try again." He is getting married for the fifth time.

Little boys sometimes get antsy. That is when there are ants in their pants.

The grandfather was taking a nap at his daughter's house. Her teenage son and friends came home and went into the garage and started to play their band. The grandfather woke up and asked his daughter what was that noise he heard? She said "You know that best describes their music."

It is not easy having a wizard for your father. You ask him for something and he says "Now say the magic words."

A boy was playing touch football with his friends. When his Mother asked how it went. He said it was touch and go.

A boy always took advantage of his younger brother. They would flip a coin and he would say heads I win and tails you lose.

A little boy said he didn't like it when his Mother called him a skunk. She said I didn't call you a skunk. You called me a stinker.

In Idaho many children want Mr. Potato Head for Christmas.

Pest control people like to buy creepy crawlers for their kids.

My grandfather is into drones. He drones on and on.

The new ice cream shop features over a hundred different flavors. A grandfather bought his grand daughter to the shop. She studied and studied the board. He said you have to make up your mind. She choose vanilla.

Our dad who was a policeman thought us kids were so bad when we were growing up. We had our pictures taken and he hung them up and called them our mug shots.

A boy got a job mowing the house on the corner lot. He promised them that he would cut the corners.

It was Christmas eve and the three small children refused to go to bed. They were told that Santa would't come if they didn't get to bed, but no matter what they told them the children refused to go to bed. Finally the father whispered something to the Mother. In a little while they heard noise on the roof. Mother says Santa is here quick get to bed because he won't come in if you are not asleep. They quickly ran upstairs and went to bed. In a little while they heard a bang, a crash, some shouting and a scream. They started to run down the stairs, but mother said that Santa's sleigh just fell off so go back to bed. She said she would check on Santa. The kids didn't understand why the next day their Dad's leg was in a cast.

A couple was saying they didn't know what they could count on anymore. Their little boy said he counts on his fingers.

First music Chinese children learn to play on the piano is chopsticks.

A wife with five children says she feeds the hungry every day. At her house they have no idea what leftovers are.

A child standing alone on a poster. Of course it is the poster child.

A man's Uncle always wanted to lots of security and a sense of belonging. I asked did he find it? He said yes he is in the State Prison.

A lady was visiting the boy's Mother. The boy asked the lady to stick out her tongue. Billy, his mother said, you don't ask people to do that He said he just wanted to see it. Mom you said she has a sharp tongue.

A seamstress tells her children she can always patch things up.

Mom made a cake. She has four children. The three younger ones came home from school while the older one was home earlier. She told them to have some cake. There was no cake. The older boy said "I can't believe I ate the whole thing".

My aunt used to be a hat maker. When she got upset we would call the Mad Hatter.

Boy to Mamma "There is a wolf at the door. What shall I tell him?" "Tell him we finished the pig yesterday".

Child on swing yells for her mother to push her. Mother says I don't like to be pushy.

My cousin had to take a dense test to see how dense he really is.

When you have twins and a problem, it is usually a twin problem.

My brother is a born leader. It is too bad he could never get anyone to follow him.

Wife telling that when their children were small when they went on trips they always camped. Her husband was too cheap to pay for a hotel room.

My brother was sent to the penitentiary. Someone said to survive he going to have to live by his wits. I said he is not going to make it.

A Mother said to her son that he needed a higher purpose in life than to see how much he can annoy his sisters.

My dad is becoming like the big stores. He is getting super sized.

Unfortunately when your college student child says they have pulled an all nighter, it doesn't necessarily mean they were studying.

Grandfather was pleased to hear that his grandson attended a party college. He was glad to see him interested in politics. He only wondered what party he was in.

The concert was loud and noisy, and not very good. A grandfather knew his grandson would want him to say something positive about the concert. So when he asked him what he thought about it. The grandfather said well I don't think anyone went to sleep during it.

The man from the electric company said he loved it when in raising his children he could say "lights out."

Son of a CIA agent first words were "I spy."

A lady, her husband and three young children were riding in a car. She was talking on the phone to a friend. Suddenly there was noise in the car as the family was arguing. She put the phone down and said "Quit fussing, you have to learn to share". The friend she was talking to said " Thats kids for you". She said "What kids I was talking to my husband".

My Mother must have loved bees. She called everyone honey and was dripping with sweetness.

The news was that an elderly lady had lost her home. The news they didn't tell you that she was bossy, controlling and had a very bad disposition. The problem was that she is my mother-in-law and moving in with us. I may be in the market for an apartment.

A mother doing too much baking and cooking can become stir crazy.

Nothing was going right with the kids. I expected them to behave in a certain way and was usually disappointed. My friend said I need to have my expectations really low so if they do the right thing it will exceed my expectations.

Mother worked in a store where she was on her feet everyday. At night she would go home and soak her feet. Her son worked in an office where he had to think hard every day. At night he tried to soak his head.

When push comes to shove I pushed my brother into the pool.

My brother's friend is an accident waiting to happen. He is always saying he is going to crash at my brother's house.

My cousins are finally spending some time together. They are locked up in the same jail.

A firefighter goes to a family reunion. Everyone likes it when he is there because he helps put out the small fires.

A boy loved to fish and have others over to tell his stories to.
His Mother had her hooks in him.
She said don't be telling fish tales out of school.
You just keep bobbing along, but there are times you need to put a cork in it.
Don't be trying to lure your friends into believing everything you tell them.
Sometimes the fish you caught was about the same size as the bait.
The fish that got away through the net because it was so small.
And don't get me started on fly fishing. You have no idea how many flies are out there on the lake.
Most of the time the only thing you caught was a sunburn.

My cousin was a star gazer. She would watch movie stars all the time.

A mother had a positive attitude about her five year old. When he wrote on the wall instead of getting upset she would say he is going to be a writer.

A couple was looking up a second cousin they didn't know very well. The wife said something is wrong we are at a prison. This can't be right. The husband said well someone said he lives in a gated community.

A man said his brother-in-law always had to top him. One time he was on a jury. Later his brother-in-law got on a jury too but he was on a grand jury.

His parents knew he was going to be a runner. Even when he was little he ran off all the time.

His father was a gardener. When they were growing up and did something bad, he would nip it in the bud.

An older man who was a widower, was asked by his daughter where he wanted to eat on a Sunday. He said Cracker Barrel. She said you know how crowed that place is on Sunday we will have to wait for over an hour to get seated. He said he was okay with that. When they got there he settled into a rocking chair and started to complain and complain. He kept it up until they were seated. His daughter asked if he knew what was going to happen why did he complain. He said "Honey I love to complain".

People always said my no good cousin would never go anywhere or amount to anything. Boy were they wrong. Just this past Christmas he got transferred from one prison to another.

A man in the army said he learned to march first when he was growing up. He would do something wrong and his Mother would say you march right up to your room.

A cattleman getting after his son says he is going to tan his hide.

A problem child is growing up. His mother said we have a rapidly growing problem.

The calm before the storm is that period of time before the relatives all descend on you for the holidays.

I don't know what happened in our family when the boys all ended up with big heads.

A parent scolded their child for being so negative. He was told to be more positive. The next day he came home and said "I am positive I failed the test today."

Parents were talking about how bad the shape of the world is in. Their young son asked "Isn't it still round?"

Whenever we would say or do some acting our mother would always make a big production out of it.

A lady died who had been a seamstress. The obituary said she was the thread that held the family together.

As the family was going to church the mother noticed that the flowers on the side of the house really needed watering. When they came home the little boy was on the side of the house. She yelled out what are you doing? He was peeing on the flowers. He said Mom I irrigated them.

The banker's son was running around like loose change.

A dairy farmer's mother-in-law came to visit and stayed to long, that the cream even soured.

My mother always wanted me to be concerned about the underwear I wore. She would say it doesn't count so much what is on the outside but what is underneath.

Two teenage boys were at the home of one of their fathers. The father expressed concern that his son stayed up late and wasn't getting enough sleep.

He said he had been reading that you need eight hours of sleep when you go to school. His son's friend said don't worry Dad your boy gets his eight hours of sleep if you count the three he sleeps at school.

A landscaper was the first to use the word "grounded" when he punished his child.

The gardeners kids were getting rather bored working in the garden. When he went back to check on them they had made somethings round with a hole in it and were shooting peas at each other. There you have it folks the story of the original pea shooter.

It was the clock maker who came up with the punishment for children called time out.

A clockmaker's son was upsetting to his father. He did everything counter clock wise. The one clockmaker said his son was so lazy. He always had time on his hands.

A dog had been staying at their house for awhile and didn't seem to belong to anyone. The boy of the house kept having kids over to look at the dog. One day the dog ran off. The boy was so upset. The father said he was just a mutt and they could get another one. The boy said you don't understand. I was charging the kids to see the flea circus on him.

A man who works at sea world when his little boy cries tells him to quit your whaling.

A wizard was trying to teach his son something and he wasn't getting it. Finally the wizard says "Do I have to spell it out for you?"

My stepchildren age me. Even though I am not a grandparent they call me gramps.

The landscaper said to his misbehaving child "Plant your butt over on the chair."

A coal miner gets after his son. He says he is going to rake him over the coals.

A bee farmer told his kids to make a bee line to the house.

A carpet layer calls his kids rug rats.
An insurance salesman is disappointed that his daughter dances in a club without much clothes. The salesman offered her full coverage.

Overheard an older man talking to a younger man saying he didn't like the way he treated his daughter. I asked if he was her boyfriend. He said no he was her doctor.

A grandson said to his grandmother that he was bored. She said when she was little and bored they used to play board games. He said are those games for people who are bored?

A landscaper says that his son's hair is bushy and needs to be trimmed.

When a fisherman was little and he would feel sorry for himself his mother would tell him to go out into the garden and eat worms. That is how he got to like them. Now when he eats grub, we are talking about grub worms.

Tommy said his family went to a farm this summer and while there they laughed and laughed. When asked why he said it was a funny farm.

When a weather mans' children act up he says they are kicking up a storm.

Mother expecting company asks her son to pass the plates to her. He asks why we aren't in church.

The grandfather had died. His prayer service was at the funeral home. The next day his body had to be brought to the church for the funeral. It turned out there was a major accident and they were late getting there. The grandmother said to her daughter, "I told him he would be late getting to his own funeral."

The teenage daughter bought those jeans in style that have holes in them. When their grandmother came to visit she didn't know what to think about them. She ended up sewing patches on them.

A seamstress said her son is kind of like a loose thread that doesn't know where he belongs.

At a family gathering the large uncle told his small nephew that one day he would grow up and be like him. The nephew ran to his father crying. "Do I have to grow as big as Uncle Dan?"

The organ player tells his noisy children to pipe down.

An astronomer would like nothing better than for his daughter to be a star. He thinks his son in so bright that he has taken to wear sunglasses when he is around him.

My daughter is a flower child who will soon start to bloom.

We all have roles to play in life. One lady said she wishes in her family she wasn't always cast as the villain.

The lady's elderly father came to stay with them. She thought it would be nice to give him the job of walking the dog. That way he could exercise and meet the neighbors. He complained that the neighbors were very unfriendly. Some asked that he not walk that way anymore. They were even getting phone calls complaining about him. The lady suggested that maybe the father should take the dog scooper and a bag with him next time he walked the dog.

A teenage boy was telling his mother about the dumb things he had done at school. He said he had done so many dumb things lately and didn't know what was wrong. His mother said "Honey you can't help you got your brains from her Dad's side.

The younger of the two boys went running to his Mother telling her that his big brother had kicked him. When the Mother asked the older son why he did it. He said before his Dad left in the morning he said "Don't lay a hand on him."

Son says he doesn't understand why his Dad gets all nervous and worked up when he has to give him a talk. He said I really don't listen to him anyway. Boy without a father says to his friend's father. "You are just like a Dad to me. By the way can I borrow twenty dollars?"

Who said it is a dirty job but someone has to do it? Parents of two college age children who have been home all summer and now went back to school. We are talking about cleaning their rooms.

A family day at the beach
Our teenage son Ben clammed up and wouldn't talk.
My wife kept giving out pearls of wisdom all day.
Our little girl looked at all the sand and said boy our cat would love this. He wouldn't know where to go to the bathroom.
We ate our picnic lunch. What's a little sand in your food anyway?
Our little girl wanted Ben to help build a sand castle but he refused saying it reminded him too much of work.

Our girl saw a turtle and watched it. She said it reminded her of Ben. They are both kind of slow.

My wife asked me what was wrong with me. She said you are turning so red. Are you upset?

Ow and more ow. I had the worst sunburn. Oh the fun of a day at the beach.

I knew my son was going to be a great bowler. Even at an early age he was always knocking things over.

It is difficult having a weatherman for a father. His head is always in the clouds. You ask him for advice and he says he hasn't the foggiest idea. He always wants you to save your money for a rainy day.

Another child said his weatherman father taught him a lot.

When he would get excited about something his dad would tell him to chill.

When he was going to do something or go somewhere without thinking his Dad would say "Freeze."

When he would tell him something that wasn't quite true his dad would say "I don't want a snow job."

When he was gloomy and overcast his Dad would tell him he wanted to see a little more sunshine.

He said "Don't let a little rain ruin your day."

He said it is my job to help prepare for for the storms of life.

If you don't listen and get hit by lighting it is not my fault.

There was a family gathering at our house. The big chair with a cushion in it was saved for Grandpa to sit in. He came in and sat down. There were noises in his seat when he sat down. Mom yelled at Tommy. "I told you to put that whoopee cushion away. Tommy said " I did Mom."

When I was growing up I used to fight with an older kid. He quite often knocked me to the ground. You could say I looked up to him.

We were eating at the Aunt's house. She is not the best cook. My little boy said to me "Mom I prayed over the food, but it still doesn't taste good.

My sister's husband Frank was always complaining and upset about something. He ruined many a family gathering and trips they went on. They were going on a trip where they would be gone for two weeks. She was worried how her sister was going to get along. After five days she got a postcard from her sister saying everything is great having a good time. When her sister got back she went and over to confront her sister and asked if her husband hadn't stayed home.

Food/Eating Out

I asked the waitress what made the hamburger a Hawaiian burger. She did the hula for me.

What breakfast food started in England? Cheerios

Why are the Chinese people the only ones that claim their food? All food eaten in China is Chinese food.

A waitress called her manager and said she couldn't come in because she was sick. He asked her what was wrong. She said it was something she ate that upset her stomach. He asked where she ate. She said it was at work yesterday.

The fruit in the store they sell that wives tell their husbands is honey do.

Where can you work hard all day and still come home smelling good. a bakery

One guy said he orders his meat like his boss said he does his job that is well done.
The other guy said he orders his meat like his boss says he does his job and that is rare. His boss says it is rare when he gets it right.
I told them I just hope your boss doesn't give you a raw deal.

Sugar sugar I have been seeing too much of you. Now I am afraid you will be seeing more of me.

In honor of super bowl Sunday they have renamed the movie "The Big Chill" to "The Big Chili."

Don't eat at the pie shop. I heard the owner has his fingers in too many pies.

If you eat to many peppers and too much spicy food you may be called "Hot Lips."

The cafe was located in an area where there were lots of hunters. They used to offer wild game on their menu. They had to quit because they weren't finding enough road kill

Dairy farmer works with the egg farmer and they came up with the idea of eggnog for Christmas.

When the cook expresses his philosophy he always says it boils down to.

The name of the new skydivers cafe is "The Do Drop Inn."

A man said he can only cook under pressure. You could say he is a pressure cooker.

What a waiter wants to hear is that someone has a big tip for him.

A lunch place worked with the box place. Together they provided box lunches.

There is a new place opening up called "The Thin Chicken."
Now I ask you who wants to eat a malnourished chicken that doesn't have any meat on its bones. There was definitely slim picking at the restaurant.

I like to eat oatmeal in the morning. Then later in the day I can feel my oats.

A couple was arguing about what to eat. She wanted a salad and he wanted an egg. They invented the egg salad.

The sign in the dinner said kids eat free on Sunday. I know I am over sixty but I am still a kid at heart so I asked if I could qualify. He said sure as long as I bring along another adult. I promised that I would act very childish.

A sanitation worker said he has been having problems eating junk food.

Restaurant workers go to a party.

One is a good mixer and can easily mix with others.

Another one tries to blend in with whatever crowd he is with.

A third stirs up the pot by saying controversial things.

A fourth offers leftovers. Leftover jokes and stories that everyone has already heard.

A fifth picks up little crumbs of conversation here and there.

To get the sixth one to talk is like scrapping the bottom of a pan.

The last one acts crazy like a cracked pot.

The question should not be "What is cooking?" but "Who is cooking?"

When a hungry man wants food he says "feed me." When he is full he say he is "fed up."

They had to fire a worker at the donut shop. He was trying to fill in the holes.

The special at the breakfast house in honer of the Pope was Eggs Benedict.

At the salad bar someone got sick. He tossed his salad.

A miner likes to eat at the Hard Rock Cafe.

Her husband was so cheap he never wanted to eat out and if they did he would buy one meal and they would split it. One time she found a place to eat that said if you buy one meal you can get the second one free, so they went there. Of course, he made her leave half of her meal so they could get a doggy bag and take it home to have another meal. He was upset that she made him leave a two dollar tip. As they left to go to their car, a man with a gun jumped by behind them. He said give me your wallet. She said you won't want what little is in there. He said shut up and give me the wallet, so the man did. Sure enough there was all of six dollars in there. I am sure the robber was thinking he had made a mistake. Than the man told the robber he wanted his wallet back. The wallet was probably worth more than the money. He started arguing with the man saying don't tale cheap shots at me. He said I know more about being cheap than you do. The wife thought maybe we should have stayed home.

A barbecue house asked the famous grill master to come and talk. They asked how he got to become a grill master. He said after being grilled by the police so many times he was an expert at it.

A baker up North where it is really cold in the winter, the first thing he put on in the morning was his long johns. Later when baking he came up with an idea for a new roll he named "long johns".

We were studying the menu at a restaurant the other day. The manager came by and picked up the menus. He said there has been a change in menus.

A dairy farmer and a corn farmer got together and came up with the idea of cream corn.

A kitchen aide was fired. She just couldn't dish it out.
A lady was bringing a pineapple cake to a party. Her cousin was driving her. Her cousin was a fast and not to careful with her driving. They kept hitting bumps on the road and finally hit one so big that the cake turned over. She didn't know what to do. When they got to the party she said her cake was an upside down pineapple cake.

A guy was at the grocery store without a cart. I told him you have to be carted to shop here.

A man in the candy department of a grocery store said he always tries to pick out a candy that reminds him of his wife. I asked what he got and he said candy corn.

The other day there were ants in the kitchen on the floor eating popcorn that I had spilled. Isn't that cute they wanted to eat the same snacks as we do.

A cattleman's first words when he eats out is "Where is the beef?"
A feminist took over the Burger King eating places. There was an overthrow of the King. Now they are called Burger Queen.

A man said his wife is a light eater. In eating a five course dinner she could only finish the first two.

Three young women were eating out. They noticed a handsome man standing at the front of the restaurant. One went over and started fanning him. He asked her what that was all about. She said her friends told her they thought he was hot.

A very attractive lady worked in a meat market. Many of the men's heads would turn to stare at her. One day two men were staring at her. She said gentlemen please this is not a meat market.

We remember the cheese on the moon, but we often forget those moon pies.

When a waiter is sick and not at work the manager says his server is down.

A man eating out was not happy with the food. He told the waiter you said the food was good. The waiter said you misunderstood. I said I was good.

I didn't know baseball players were such big eaters. But than I read that they are always stepping up to the plate.

A waiter complains after the two firemen ate they left him a hot tip.

Down South the potatoes are nicer than up North. They are called sweet potatoes in the South.

There was trouble at the breakfast house. The cook was overcooked and steamed poured out of his ears. He was being hard boiled. All egg orders were turning out eggs over hard. Nobody was cracking up. The waitress said he has quite the distemper when angry. You have to walk on egg shells around him. Whatever you do don't egg him on.

When things are looking good the weatherman says to the waitress "Hello Sunshine, I want my eggs sunny side up."

It was named Hooters because the owner liked owls.

The Chinese may have invented the egg roll, but the chicken farmer is the one that came up with the idea of the egg toss.

Where the smell is good and it makes you hungry, but you are usually disappointed. It is quite often the school lunch.

I order a wrap sandwich and it wasn't good so I had to send it back. It was a bad wrap.

Customer to waitress asks what smells so good. The waitress says we keep our back door open so we can get the smells from the bakery next door.

Customer complaining to waitress says he can't eat his food. The waitress says she will bring him a doggy bag.

The pizza place says their pizza is so good it like you are not just getting a slice of pizza but a slice of life.

History

He was such a happy rancher. When he died his children wanted to honer him. They named the candy "jolly ranches" for him.

Whistlers drink a lot of liquid because they always need to wet their whistle.

Who says "the vultures are circling?" A man who just won the lottery and his relatives found out.

Years ago in one area in Africa there were plenty of bushes, but few bathrooms. When they had to go they were told to find a bush. To this day they are called the bush people. In some areas there were very few bushes. Than a bush pilot had to fly over the area to look for bushes. When he found one he marked it on a map. That was called an oasis.

Two guys are working in a sandwich shop. Their shift is about over. The one guy is always experimenting with the sandwiches putting different things around the meat. The other guy says, "Our dates are waiting we have tickets to a concert. Just call it a wrap and let's go". There you have it folks the history of the wrap sandwich.

A judge takes off his robe that is where we get the term disrobe from.

Mary worked in a bar and was always getting cut and then she would bleed. They liked her so much they called her "Bloody Mary" and named a drink after her.

The cowboys would always ride off into the sunset. Do you have any idea how hard that was on their eyes. Plus they had so many accidents. Finally a man came up with the idea and that is when sunglasses were invented.

What dwarf had allergy problems? Sneezy

What animal's shoes are thrown everywhere? Horse

A cowboy had his horse bring his girlfriend a gift in the horse's mouth. The girl looked at the horse, and the horse dropped the package and bite her. That is where we get the saying "Don't look a gift horse in the mouth."

In the old West when there was a problem they could always call in the calvary.

I didn't know we have a holy city in the United States. It is Holy Toledo.

In the old West the Indians sometimes had trouble with the smoke signals. Sometimes the signals got mixed up and a war started. It was difficult to get the communications straight. If they put too much wood on the fire instead of saying something peaceful it might end up meaning "I am going get you sucker."

The most dangerous tree in the old West was called the hanging tree.

The first Indians were eager to learn. One of the first words they asked was "How."

The first men to be go clubbing were cave men. If you had more material things than another cave man you might live in a cave by the sea.

You know how the mad cow disease started? Some teenagers would go into the pasture and tip cows over. If you got tipped over you would be a mad cow too.

We don't often hear the stories about those famous cowards of society who had a yellow streak. When Paul Revere was busy warning people that the British were coming Samuel Johnson was busy packing his belonging and heading the opposite way. During the famous Boston Tea Party Patrick Jackson didn't throw away all his tea. He kept some back and was later seen having tea with some British soldiers. When it was time to cross the Delaware, Joseph Kane told Washington that riding in the boat made him sick and thus he never crossed the Delaware.

Why was an outhouse called an outhouse? Because it was outside.

I don't know how old the man is who is called the "Whistler" because he whistles all the time. Nobody can remember his real name. I know he is old because I have seen a picture of Whistler's mother.

It used to be people just lived in poverty. Now with all the credit cards they no longer live just in poverty but in debt.

Have you ever wondered why so many bad guys were found out West in the early 1800's. When they got in trouble back East, the law would say I want you on the next stagecoach headed West.

In the days of knights do you ever think how hard it would be to change into something more comfortable or even go to the bathroom?

Many a pioneer woman is responsible for the starting of many small towns and cities around the country. The pioneer men had a restless spirit and the women would tell them it was time for them to settle down.

In the army there was a row of urinals in the men's bathroom. The one who cleaned got so disgusted because there was always pee on the floor. He finally put a sign on top of the urinals that said "Aim higher."

Tap dancing was first started in the West. When someone starts shooting at your feet you lear to tap dance pretty fast.

In the old West the bad guys ate a lot. They would always say "Let's rustle up some grub.

You know how they identified the smallest town out West. It was called a one horse town.

When they say someone has fallen off the wagon. It means they have gone back to drinking.

A guy's pants are sagging. Cowboy says "Son you may want to hitch up your britches we don't want to be seeing your moon".

When cowboys go somewhere they always mosey on over.

If a cowboy wore his pants low he was called a low rider.

Two things bothered the cowboy. One was saddle sores from being in the saddle so much. The other thing they had to watch out for was the snakes and not to get too rattled.
When their was a team of hoses often they were impatient and wanted to take off. The one cowboy said to the other cowboy you need to hold your horses.

If the horse could pull a lot it was called horse power.

Sometimes the cowboys would race their horses and people felt they weren't safe in the streets. That is when they put up the sign "No horsing around."

They were painting but forgot their brushes. This was the start of finger painting.

They were gentleman in the old West. They would tip their hat and say "Yes ma'm as soon as I am done eating I will take my six shooter and take care of that varmint for you.

In Africa when they would communicate with drums. One drum beat off could change the whole course of the conservation.

A knight's wife said he was her knight in shining armor.

It was not easy raising your children for the cave dwellers. First you had to get after them for throwing rocks at the neighbors and their children. Than all they wanted to do was go rock climbing, and you were forever yelling at them to get down. Then when the parents were gone there was the writing and drawing pictures on the cave walls. That is where they got the first pictures of cave dwellers. It was from naughty children.

It was going to be a big day for the museum. Someone had found in an attic an original flag from the Civil War. They hadn't seen the flag yet it was in a box. They wanted to give it privately to the museum. The museum would have none of that. They made a big fuss about it and invited everyone that was anyone to the museum to see the flag. At the end of the ceremony the box was opened, and the flag taken out, it was a white flag. The letter with it explained they were surrounded and saw no way out so that is when they raised the white flag.

The wife of the cave dweller complained about all the stones around. Her husband said "You know in looking back some day they will call this "The Stone Age." His wife did get a better attitude and even started a rock garden. Their son was the first "Stoner."

Back in my day when they wanted to clean the floors they had a sock hop. In the old West if you were told to get off your high horse the only thing you could do was dismount and get off.

During the time of the gladiators they had to whip them into shape.

A miner had a deep love of his Mother. When he found a large uranium deposit he named it for his Mother. It was called the Mother load.

An Indian man was the first one to win the salesman of the year award. He sold the same bridge to the Pilgrims three times.

The Indians were also the first pacifists. They would smoke the peace pipe. When their mother in law came and she was on the warpath that peace pipe was used quite a bit.

The Indian children knew they were in for trouble when their Dad called them to a pow wow.

Law/Courts

What number lawyers and bartenders like is the fifth.

A female judge says it is hard not to be a judge. At home she is married to a pastor. He has a sign in the kitchen that says "Thou Shalt Not Judge."

They wanted me to stand in line. I said I hate to stand in line. They wanted me in the lineup at the police station.

A judge who married wrong you could say he had poor judgement.

A detective should not marry a cleaner. She dusts for fingerprints and he looks for fingerprints.

A person high up in the political realm had been arrested. He had lawyered up and wasn't talking. The police put him in a small room and turned the heat up. They told him that his mother-in-law who hated him was going to question him. The papers reported that he was beginning to feel the heat and starting to sweat it out.

A lawyer was divorcing his wife. He thought of her as a liability. She thought of him as a trial lawyer and being married to him was a trial.

When a cop falls into the mud, he is called a dirty cop.

I was concerned if she was earning her money legally because she told me she was on a fixed income.

A detective was interviewing suspect in the woods. An owl flew bye and said "Who." The detective looked around and said "If it is okay with you I will ask the questions around here.

A banker on the witness stand in a fraud case
I suppose you want my statement.
Don't be daft I never overdraw money.
I just hope you don't lose your interest in the case.
I couldn't have met him on that date you say because that is a banker's holi-
day.
You know I am on a roll today.
Yes I gave him the prime rate.
I know you want to know where the money has gone to. I suggest you look at
my lawyer, he certainly has a large share of it.

Judge to defendant "If you are innocent than you need to wipe that guilty look
off your face."

There was a robbery in a bookstore. A lady in the corner had been sitting
there reading a book. When the detective asked her what she saw, she said
she couldn't see much. But the detective said you had your glasses on. Yes,
but you see these are my reading glasses.

The judge says to the man in a lawsuit case, "I would appreciate it if you put
your pants back on. I know you want to demonstrate how he is suing the pants
off of you."

The policeman was sent out to tail a suspect and where he went. The suspect
went to the mall to shop. The policeman decided so he wouldn't stand out he
would do a little Christmas shopping too. They went from store to store. The
captain asked than what happened? Well we were in different lines paying for
our stuff, and wouldn't you know it I got stuck in the slow line and lost him.

When guards get old they are called the old guard.

A bail bondsman may have gone beyond his boundaries. He as developed a
special bond with some of his clients.

A man is about to be given the oath on the witness stand. He says stop. Now if I have to tell the truth I will probably get in trouble. My wife already thinks I have a big mouth. I promised her I would not tell on her. She gave me a list of what to say and what not to say.

Three young guys robbed a store. The alarm went off they raced out and two made it to the car where they took off. The third was caught. They left him holding the bag.

A man said he could earn some money but what he would be doing would not be quite legal. He told his wife it would be like taking dirty money. She said you could bring it home and she would wash it.

In court the witness was being questioned. It is true that you were standing right behind the defendant who is accused of taking a valuable ring? Yes sir. Can you describe what you saw? I was at the store to get rings for me and my fiancee. I was looking at him, until the door opened and this beautiful lady came in. I am afraid after that I couldn't take my eyes off of her, so I don't remember seeing anything else.

Middle aged jury member in the jury room talking. Did you see the way the defendant smiled at me? Surely he couldn't be guilty. I think he even winked at me. Myrtle another jury member said he is on trial for taking advantage of women.

A young guy in his early twenties was taken down to the police station for questioning. They also searched him. When they were done his mother was waiting outside the room for him. He said they found him clean. His mother a clearer said I know I taught you well.

An ex con said he would be a good marriage candidate. He has already been tried and tested.

A defendant in court claims he didn't do what he was charged with. The lawyer says it is getting disgusting that nobody wants to take the credit for anything anymore.

An ex con is running for office on his record.

Man in court was asked why he stole the dog collar. He said it was dark and it was an honest mistake. He was trying to reach for a necklace.

The witness was going to testify on the stand. He had a low monotone voice. Sure enough before he was done they had to wake up three of the jurors and the judge had started to nod off.

A man had died suddenly at a banquet right after they had desert. The detectives were investigating. One said he felt for sure it was poison but there was no proof. The younger detective whispered to him that the proof was in the pudding.

A lawyer said the only way I can get to tell the truth is to have his mother come by. He can tell her his story and you know I don't think he can look her in the eye and tell a lie.

The defense attorney tells the defendant to try and tell the story again but with a straight face. He said last time when all the jury started laughing at your story it didn't go well for you.

My uncle likes to surround himself with people who think the same way he does. A friend asks how that was working out. He found the place in the state prison.

Prisoner I wish I had gone for that limited time offer.

In court the defendant was asked questions about certain actions he had done. The defendant said he didn't want to talk about it. He asked if they could please change the conversation.

A lady judge to defendant in court says this is the fourth time I have seen you in my court this year and I don't like it. Do you have something to say for yourself. He says I don't like it either and it would be a whole lot better if we meet somewhere else.

They brought the carpenter into the police station for questions about a crime.
They tried to ply him with questions.
He felt like putty in their hands.
It was like they saw right through him.
He was beginning to come unhinged.
They tightened the screws on him.
He thought he was going to end up behind the big wall.

A man was arrested for burglary. He told his lawyer that they wouldn't find anything on him. He said before he broke into the house he washed his hands and fingers real good so he would not leave any fingerprints.

A defendant to lawyer says if the truth is told I will be going away for a long time.

Some things were missing from the kitchen at the prison. After investigating the sheriff said it looks like it was an inside job.

A defense attorney getting a defendant ready to testify. He says now look me in the eye and tell me that same lie again.

A pilot was being investigated for illegal smuggling but it was hard to catch him. So far he was flying under the radar.

Man said to the witness "I said you are a witness not that you are witless."

A pilot had been arrested but they wouldn't let him out on bail. They said he was a flight risk.

Two guys were talking. When asked what he did the one said he made records. The other guy said "Really I do the same. I have a long record at the police station".

The judge and the math teacher both say "You are out of order."

The police arrested a naked man. After awhile they had to let him go. They couldn't find anything on him.

The foreman of the jury says can't we just all agree.

The police brought Mr. Birdman into the jail for questioning. When they were through with him he was singing like a carney.

Judge I didn't nod to give you the okay. You were going on and on and I was starting to nod off.

A perfectionist would not do good in jail. There are so many crooked people there and he would try to straighten them all out.

A man was called by his Uncle who was quite old to come down to the police station to pick him up. He was quite upset by the time he saw his Uncle. His Uncle told him to calm down. He said that two nice young officers offered him an escort downtime. They even let him ride in the back seat of their police car. They must have mistaken him for someone important because they wanted to take his picture and fingerprints. I met a man in jail who had several charges against him that would result in several trials. But he said soon all his trials would be over. I didn't want to bother the police for a ride back so I called you.

A beautiful lady was testifying on behalf of the defendant. One jury member whispered to another. She sure is a great body of evidence.

The officer stopped the man and asked if he didn't know he was speeding. He said "No sir, I was too busy texting."

The highway patrolman finally got the man to pull over. He said I clocked you at 95 miles per hour. The man said "Isn't that something. I just got this car the other day and didn't know it could go so fast."

The lawyer asked the defendant on the stand if we would swear to tell the truth and nothing but the truth. He said he would be happy to if they could get his wife and mother-in-law to leave the court room.

The defense lawyer asked the defendant why he had changed his story on the witness stand from the one he had told him earlier. He said he was locked up for awhile and he thought this story was a better story.

The alibi that all defendants want is an ironclad alibi.

The defendant told his story of what had happened. The defense attorney looked at him like he didn't believe him. The defendant said "I sure hope you don't have trust issues."

Marriage

An Hispanic man when he got married told his wife that his casa was her casa. Now after twenty years of marriage they are getting a divorce. Now he says my casa is her casa.

A cleaner loves to clean. Fortunately she married a messy man so she can clean up after him. She said the only ring he leaves her is a ring around the bathtub.

A man said to his friend that he has a lot stored in his brain. His wife added that it is mostly useless information.

A man said his wife had so many accidents. Before she could get her driver's license renewed she had to take a crash test.

A shirt says "battle tested." I asked if he had been in the military. He said no he had been married three times.

It is difficult being married to a demolition man. He gets so angry that he explodes. Than the wife feels like she is falling to pieces. Later I heard they were breaking up anyway. She said that she never knows when he is going to blow up.

When an oil man's marriage was over it was like the oil well went dry.

A lady said she wanted to marry a golfer and hoped to see green and I don't mean grass. So far she has mostly seen the grass.

In a disaster it pays to be married to a former scout. Their motto is "be prepared."

A woman said all his life her husband had worked hard to find gold. They had lived all over in gold mining areas, he spent all their money in his search, but ended up dying poor. She had him buried in a wooded box. With the money she saved on the funeral she went out and bought herself a gold ring. Well at least someone found gold.

When your married to a cleaner at least you have clean clothes to wear.
A wife of a builder complains that he is building a wall between them.

A man said his runner wife had left him. He wasn't worried. He said that one of these days she would come running back to him.

She was a driven woman. Of course it helped that her husband was a cab driver.

It was the funeral of an elderly lady whose husband was still alive. Two of her friends reached the casket where they looked at her. One said to the other "I can't believe it. That purple dress I remember when her husband gave it to her. She said to me this is so ugly, I wouldn't be caught dead in it."

I can easily read my husband's mood just by looking at his face. I would have to say he is an easy read.

The wife of an astronomer complained how messy he is. He leaves his clothes everywhere and has messes all over the house. It he belongs to a planet it is the planet of the apes.

There was a beard judging contest. To be nice to their wives they let them pick the prizes. They all got razors.

My husband is a retired ship captain. At night he snores like a fog horn.

A husband says his wife talks all the time and never shuts up. He is hoping she will have a good scare this Halloween. He is hoping she will be scared speechless.

Wife to clown husband tells him not to be acting silly around her.

A bookstore man's marriage was so short it was like just a few pages out of his life.

The wife complained to her husband that he loved the dog more than he loved her. He said it isn't his fault he has been in the doghouse so often.

A detective should marry a painter. He is a plain clothes detective and as a painter she could add some color to his life.

A man said his wife was always into helping out one cause of another. He said how about helping me. She told him he was a lost cause.

A lady said her husband has never said a cross word to her.
One lady whispered to another one that she had seen him give her the finger when she wasn't looking. Another lady said she has seen him give her the stink eye more than once.

Fishermen were talking about their wives and how they reminded them of fish. One said I divorced my wife so she is sort of like the fish that I threw back into the lake. The second said my wife is loud and mouthy sort of like a loud mouth bass. The third said his wife was like a bullhead or catfish. She is very stubborn and catty. The fourth said his wife comes from money and likes money she is like a goldfish. The fifth said his wife is like a shark very aggressive to get what she wants. They all looked at the sixth guy. He said well you know my wife likes to cook and eat. You might say she is like a whale.

A lady who married a wizard says she just came under his spell. Sometimes she needs his attention and than she tells him "I hate to break your spell, but I need to talk to you."

A woman says just because her husband is a ditch digger it doesn't mean he isn't smart. Just the other day a man was going on and on about an idea and my husband said his idea was full of holes.

Some older ladies were talking.
One said her husband was retired but still worked part time.
When asked what he did she whispered he's a spy.
The other ladies got excited and asked if he worked for the CIA or the FBI.
She said nothing that exciting. He spies on the neighbors.

An older retired man lost his voice. It happens to many older men who are not used of being at home with their wife and having to talk and shout so much.

A lady said her husband and dog do the same thing. They both chase cars. He is a highway patrolman.

A runner said when he got married his wife stopped him in his tracks. She said no more running off.

Astronomer said he was wife his morning star. Later when things were not going so good her called her his falling star.

Two electricians getting married
The couple is going to be fussed together.
Hopefully there will not be a overload at the socket.

There will be some static when they don't understand each other.

At times they will be an overcharged when one of them is really charged up.

There will be some shocks when they find out certain things about each other.

They should not abuse the power they have.

They need to know where the switch is and when to turn on or off their emotions.

Hopefully when they are married there will be a lot more light in their home.

A man named his grass for his mother-in-law. He called it crab grass.

The wife was married to an astronomer. He used to gaze at the starts in her eyes when he was first in love. Now he just gazes at the stars in the sky.

A man comes home late at night. His wife is waiting for him. He starts to her a long story. She puts her hand up and says stop. I don't want to hear the story I just want the facts. He says you are no fun, now I am not sure I can tell you anything.

A man said his wife was a doll. One man said his wife was like a porcelain doll, she breaks easy. The other man said his wife is like a cry baby. The fourth man it is worse for me my wife is like a doll that cries "Mamma" all the time.

When they got married she loved him for his wavy brown hair.

Now many years have past and thing have changed.

Their marriage is in trouble.

His hair and his wife have had a falling out.

A man said his wife feels she is so important. He keeps a set of drums in the living room. When she comes in he gives her a drum roll.

A wife who's husband is a detective asked him when he came home why his hands were so cold. He said he had been working on cold cases all day.

A lady said she divorced her husband. When the attractive widow lady moved in next door he took the saying "love your neighbor to heart."

A man and his wife had so many fights mostly about her being late to everything. If they went to a movie they always missed the first part. If they went to a party they had trouble parking because everyone else was already there. They always missed the music at church and if they went to a play an usher had to show them to their seats in the dark. After forty years of marriage to celebrate they decided to go on a cruise. After they had been gone a few days their friends got a post card from the husband. It said having a wonderful time, the trip is everything they said it would be and more. P.S. my wife missed the boat.

An uncle doesn't treat his wife the same. When they travel he flies first class and sends her in coach.

The lady says her policeman husband is such a poor reader that the only time he read is when he reads someone their rights.

My wife is terrible cook. At our house you don't want to know what is cooking.

The weather man got married in a hurry. It was whirlwind romance.

A husband and wife were arguing. He said I know I am right because I read it in a book. She yells back the book was probably fiction.

Some wives treat their husbands like babies. After a fight they expect them to come crawling back to them.

Math teacher to husband I have told you 153 times not to throw your clothes on the floor, but use the hamper. Math teachers count everything.

A music teacher said her husband was just to low key. There was no harmony in their home and they couldn't seem to find the right chord. They ended up singing different tunes, and she didn't like his tone when he talked to her. On that note she left him.

Two cleaners got together. It was a spotless relationship.

A junkyard man and his wife were having some serious problems. He was trying to salvage what he could of their marriage.

There is something new in nagging. Now your wife can nag you without seeing you. Aren't cell phones wonderful? They're used for nonstop nagging.

A husband was busy paying the bills. He told his wife if they were going for broke they were already there.

Wife to her pest control husband. I really wish when we go out you would wear something that doesn't smell like bug spray. I don't appreciate all the bugs following us.

A baker said her husband is like a sponge cake.

A lady said in earlier life someone must have told her husband not to move a muscle, because throughout the years he sure hasn't.

It is hard to be married to someone in show business. Every time he confronts his wife about something, she gives him a song and dance routine.

A man says his wife married the right man. She is always saying what a wreck she is. He just happens to be a tow truck driver who tows wrecks.

A laundry worker is breaking up with her husband. She said there marriage is all washed up. She doesn't want to hear him spin any more tails. She doesn't want to spend another cycle with him. She is going to divorce him and drag him to the cleaners and clean him out.

It was Christmas eve. The wife opened up a big package for her. It was a fur coat. She yelled it is just what I want. She gave her husband a kiss than she modeled it forever to see it on her. Everyone was happy for her. The son said to his Dad way to go, I didn't know you knew what to get her. The Father said I never saw that coat before tonight. Oh the joys of self-giving.

When a banker and his wife went shopping he always held her hand. One clerk said isn't that sweet? The other clerk said you are kidding he does that because she is known for her shop lifting.

A plumber told his wife he was King of the house. She said okay and your throne is the toilet seat.

A couple were visiting with another couple. The man said I know the answer is in the back of my mind. His wife told the other couple "You don't know how much clutter is back there.

A husband called his wife his little Honey Bun. Every Christmas he would get her clothes. The clothes were all three sizes too small. She would get excited and whisper to everyone and say "Isn't it cute that my husband thinks I am so small." A few days after Christmas she would take the clothes back and exchange them. The thing was that she never knew that her husband knew her correct size.

My husband is like a shoe, a loafer.

My wife is spending so much time working on beads she is getting beady eyes.

A carpenter's wife has given up on him and left him to his own vices.

An older man heard his wife talking on the phone to their friend Frank. He asked his wife if Frank said he was a peacemaker. She said no Frank said he got a pacemaker.

An older man was bragging to another man telling him war stories. His wife said to the other wife the only war he was in was probably a pillow fight and he may have lost that. He has definitely lost the battle of the bulge and the battle of the mind.

A dog lover wants to stay in bed.
His wife tries to get him up.

He says he is dog tired and is going to stay in bed.
Later she checks on him and tries to get him up.
He says remember the saying "Let sleeping dogs lie."
Later his boss calls. The man asked his wife what he said.
He said if you don't show up for work you are going to be dog gone.

When your wife is a nag when she is young when she gets to be old she will be an old nag.

Wife who is shop keeper only wants to talk shop.

A couple were walking around town. She said it is so quiet here. Her husband said it should be as we are walking in the cemetery.

A bee keeper says when he thinks of his former wife he beaks out in hives.

A wife buys her clothes for her husband. He says these clothes are a size to big. She says don't worry you will grow into them.

I know my husband has some hidden assets but in the ten years we have been married, I haven't been able to find them.

A miner said his wife takes care of things that are on the surface.

A man introducing his new bride says she is the one who has brought me to my knees.

A wife finally found a job for her lazy husband. He is going to participate in a sleep study.

The weather man said he and his wife have weathered many a storm.

The carpenter said his wife can be very level headed but his mother-in-law as tough as nails.

What women at night when sleeping tell their husbands to do and often tell their dog to the same thing is to roll over.

My husband is a policeman and is always trying to get out of things. I tell him not to cop out.

Two stock brokers are getting married.
They brokered the deal.
They are bonded to each other.
They promised to share everything.
They promised not to sell short.
There are going to be a lot of returns in this marriage.

My husband a pilot is always having a good time flying high.

When both my wife and mother-in-law chew me out I get a double dosage.

When I was traveling with my wife all I saw was relatives.

Wife was talking in her sleep. The husband told her that he heard her talking. She asked what she said. He said it sounded like a private conservation and he didn't want to eavesdrop.

My husband thinks just because he is a pastor he has to have the last word. After everything is said he always adds an amen to that.

Husband got in trouble for mixing up the clothing bags. The bag that was for good-will went to the dry cleaners, while the dry cleaner clothes were given to goodwill.

My wife is such a good talker. She can usually talk herself into almost anything.

A man who works in a retail clothing store was telling his manager how bad his wife was in spending. She just wants to buy all the time and spends way more than she should. After listening awhile the manager said he could offer her some coupons. Maybe she could shop here.

A man talking to another man said he and his wife had been window shopping. The other man said that reminds him that he and his wife need to shop for drapes.

Two man were talking. The one said his wife sleeps to much. He says she is getting her beauty sleep. He says between you and me I don't think it is working.

A husband says to the new bride, " I would carry you across the threshold, but I am afraid my back would go out."

A couple said they have been so busy they have to set time aside to fight.

My husband believes he evolves from the monkeys. I promised the kids I would take them to the zoo to see the rest of his relatives.

My wife does a lot of critical thinking when it comes to me.

A wizard said his wife was charming as usual.

He worked at the zoo. His wife said he was a keeper.

My husband thinks he is royalty. When he's out with the guys he thinks he is a prince among men.

My Aunt believes there is a place for everything and everything has to be in a place. When she got married she immediately put her husband into his place.

I think my husband is trying to get rid of me. He knows how allergic I am to cats. Yesterday he brought a big cat home.

Even if a cleaning lady get a divorce, she doesn't want a messy divorce. She wants a clean break.

The wife of a fireman says that sometimes to get him moving she has to start a fire under him.

My husband is a gambler but even when the chips are down I still love him.

My husband likes to play basketball. Both the ball and his head are inflated.

His wife was an excellent cook. She left him. A friend asked how he was doing. He said okay, but I wish she hadn't left me on a empty stomach.

A wife could never get her husband to notice her. One day she went out and got her hair dyed bright red. She came home anxious to surprise him. She said to him well do you notice anything different? He was busy watching television and reading the paper. He looked over her and said "It looks like you forgot to get our lunch."

My husband bring home our food every night. It pays to be married to a pizza delivery man.

Her husband who is a trucker has a high opinion of himself. He thinks of himself as the King of the Road.

I tell husbands to buy my joke book than your wife can laugh at the jokes instead of you.

My wife likes to be in fashion. Even going to a party she is fashionably late.

Man to wife I am sorry I shrunk your sweater when I washed it. Wife says that's okay at least you didn't shrink the kids.

My husband is like a puzzle there are so many pieces to him. Over the years I have managed to put together most of the pieces, but I feel like he is missing a few pieces.

A scene between a couple that were fighting on stage. The director said there is way too much drama here.

The couple had been going through a long bitter divorce. They were fighting over everything. One day she knew the fight was over. Her husband who worked at the local post office had the white flag flying on the pole.

A man complained to his co-workers that his wife doesn't understand him. A worker said don't feel bad. None of us understand you either.

A husband is doing the cooking. Later when they eat the wife finds a hair in her food. He says that is where my hair has been going.

A pilot got married. He promised to make his wife his co-pilot. She understands that when he needs to work out problems or be alone that he will probably fly off somewhere. When he is gone he has promised to give her his flight plan and listen to the radio for messages. He has promised to give her ground control and let her make the decisions on the ground. They got married and few off. We don't know where to because they didn't leave their flight plan with anyone.

The landscaper loves his wife in an earthy way.

A birdman and his wife got a divorce. She got the house and he got the tree house.

My husband always said we would take a little trip. I never knew how little until we went one county over.

Wife works at a laundry. Her husband is a disc jockey. She hates it when he airs their dirty laundry on the air. To give her side of the story he wants her to buy air time.

A cross dresser is when your husband has to get dressed in his fancy clothes to go somewhere he doesn't want to go.

My husband doesn't like to read. I was surprised to get a call from the police station. They said he was booked.

The librarian reads too many books. Her husband said she is overbooked. She also reads too much into situations. And he hates it when she tries to read his mind.

A miner said he never found his pot of god, but instead settled for marrying a lady with a heart of gold.

Superman's wife said he may be a big man out in the world but at home he is something different. He won't lift a finger to help around the house.

An electrician and his wife split up. He was still thinking about saving energy. He told her the last one out of the house be sure to shut the lights out.

Don't be playing games with me. What the wife says to her gambling husband. When he wants to gamble more she say "no dice, and no more chips for you."

If a fireman married a weather lady there would be a firestorm.

Two older men were walking in the mall. One said "I keep hearing a shrieking high winning sound in my ear". The other man turned around and said "Fred your wife is yelling at you."

She meet her husband in a bargain basement. She said that even than he was fifty percent off.

A couple had to sell their lake cabin. The husband got cabin fever.

After his wife died a banker married the cleaning lady. It turned out to be a mistake. After a few years they got a divorce and she cleaned out his banking account.

The landscaper's wife called him on his cell phone and asked what he was doing. He said he was digging something up.

An ideal couple
She is rich and he is poor.
She wants to help the poor.
He isn't to proud to take money from her.

A man comes home late at night.
His wife meets him at the door with her night cream on and a hairnet on her
hair, in a ratty housecoat and no makeup on.
She crosses her arms and says "Well"
He says to her, "You are truly a vision of beauty".
She says "So you have been drinking again".

A ship captain in his forties was getting married for the first time. It is sort of
like sailing in uncharted waters.

Before my actress wife tells a story she always has to set the stage.

The weather man said he can tell when his mother-in-law is coming, she al-
ways brings a cold front.
He said to her look what the wind blew in.
It is going to be a stormy night.
He could feel a chill in the air.
She kept throwing lighting rods at him hoping to strike down whatever he said.
He said his goodwill towards her was melting.

A man said he was in the dog house so much he built a larger one but with
heat and air-conditioning.

A pool player said he was so good they even named a building after him. It is
called the pool hall. His wife liked to play pool too. She knew her cue and
sometimes she would take a stick to him. She put in her side pocket her
winnings.

A lady said she was working to get her husband up to date.
Another lady said her husband is so out of date.

Another said what her husband does is so dated.

The fourth lady said well the way my husband is I don't even have to make any dates to write on the calendar.

I asked the young woman how she ended up marrying the banker. Her mom's advice was to follow the money.

Men were complaining that their wives were always borrowing things and than expecting them to return the items for them. One said that isn't so bad. He said his wife is always borrowing trouble and you can't return that.

It is hard when your husband works for the sanitation department when you take a trip. I say if you have seen one landfill you have seen them all.

A mortician was meeting with an older couple. They were making plans for the man's funeral. When they got to the cost of the casket and other things the woman said that was way too expensive. The mortician looked at the man sand said what do you think? It is your funeral.

They say when you get married what is yours and what is hers becomes yours instead. You may be in trouble if one of you had a big debt.

I thought we were tight together. Later I found out what a tightwad he really was.

The groom at a wedding told the piano player it isn't necessary to play "When the Saints come marching in" when the bride's family enters.

An older man had his hearing tested. The doctor said there is nothing wrong with your hearing. He said "Don't tell my wife, I haven't been listening to her in years."

My wife is a detail person. She not only wants to know the story but all the details connected to it.

I gained so much weight because my wife had to sugar coat everything she said to me.

It is hard to impress your wife when you own a junkyard. She looks around and says this is just junk.

I wanted peace of mind but my mother-in-law always gave me a piece of her mind.

Wife to dog loving husband. I don't like the sound of your bark.

When asked to do some work my husband is like a dog. He rolls over and plays dead.

Wife to husband who is writing his obituary. I don't think you can say you support the arts when you buy art supplies for the kids.

A couple worked in a retail store.
They were so wrapped up with each other.
They decided to tie the knot.
They were offered a package deal.
It was not hard to sell them on the deal.
When they said their vows instead of saying "I do" they said "sold."
Everyone at the wedding got coupons for discounts at the store.
At lot of good things are in store for this couple.

A hog farmer complained to his wife. She went and spent a lot of money going to a spa and having a mud bath. He said you cold have saved the money and had a mud bath with the pigs.

A book lover said she knows her husband from cover to cover.
There used to be some romance there even some mystery but now with the fights they are having it is mostly drama.

The bee keeper said when his wife hurt his feelings he felt like he had been stung.

A relator said his wife is a high price item.

An astronomer said his wife and he are so different it is like they are from different planets.
A comedian was making fun of his wife telling how dumb she is. Someone from the audience yelled she must be dumb to have married you.

A man's wife likes to shop and when she can't decide which one of two things to buy, she usually buys both.

My husband is a gambler. When we first dated he called me his good luck charm. After ten years of marriage now he says I bring him bad luck.

When a miner's wife dusts she dusts for gold dust.

I tried to stay in step with my husband, but he was always one step ahead of me.
A lady had been married to Joe Hill, but was now divorced from him for the past three years. She said she was finally over the hill.

The new vow in a marriage says "Until debt do we part."

When a weather man has been around his wife's critical sisters too much at a family gathering he says it is like being in an ice storm.

If a woman leaves a man and than goes back to him and this happens time after time the relationship is called a Yo Yo relationship.

I know my husband sometimes is in pain. I can say this he never suffers in silence.

A man said when his wife named Hope died he felt hopeless.

When A Czech man get married his wife is called his Czech mate.

A man came home late at night while his wife was in bed. This was the start of the first bedtime story. He told her a long story about why he was late. If she doesn't like the story he will find himself sleeping on the edge of the bed with no covers. In the night his wife give him a hard kick and knocks him out of bed. He yells at her. She said she had a nightmare. He says he doesn't believe her. She says he had better, it he wants her to believe the story he told her.

A lady said the only thing her magician husband can make disappear is their money.

A postal worker knew it was serious when his wife left him. She didn't leave any forwarding address.

A plumber called his wife excited about winning the pot at work. When he told his wife she got kind of quiet. Finally she said "I don't think we need another toilet seat."

The eye doctor and his wife were having marriage problems. They no longer could see eye to eye.

A man said whenever his wife and he went out she always made a big scene. He was stuck working behind the scene.

A detective's wife talked all the time. He kept reminding her that she had the right to remain silent.

A banker's wife said their arguments were always about money. Her husband had no interest in her or the children. When they wanted money he said they didn't qualify for even a loan. This marriage is headed for bankruptcy.

A plumber's wife said her husband was always concerned that she keep a tidy bowl.

She was married to a runner, but she just couldn't keep up with him.

Wife of a cab driver said her husband always had to be in the driver's seat. She sat in the backseat. If she said anything he would tell her how he hated back-seat drivers. In her marriage she was just along for the ride.

I was married to a stock broker. We had lost the special bond we once had. Now we are running out of options.

I am married to a lawyer. Anytime he gets into trouble he wants to plea bargain his way out of it. When anyone tries to tell him something he says "I object."

I am married to a doctor when I complain to him he asks me what is ailing me. He says "Have you taken your medicine today?"

Her husband is so thin. The other ladies at the club commented on it. She said that he runs all the time. They all thought that was good. She said not necessarily. He has been running from things all our married life.

My husband was always making so many funny faces. I told him he should have been a clown.

Marriage is like a pencil.
At first you both think your partner is to sharp.
A few years later you have quit writing to each other and both of you begin to think the other one is a little dull.
After a few more years you think they are getting slow and when you want to go somewhere you tell them to get the lead out.
A few more years you think you have heard everything they have to say. When they are talking to you, you say just get to the point.
If you want your marriage to last you need to keep sharping it up.

A newscaster's proposal to the weather girl.
I want to be your anchor.
I want you to get all your news from me first.
I promise to be with you rain or sunshine.
Together we can ride out all the storms of life.

86

I want to be able to broadcast that we are getting married.
There were a lot of misty eyes in the newsroom that day.

A lady went to a party without her husband. They asked why he didn't come. She had told him not to embarrass her the way he had at the last two. To be safe he just stayed home.

A carpenter's wife complained that she had a broken nail.

Her husband can't just have a cough he has to have a whopping cough.

They say the astronaut's wife is kind of spacey.

An apple grower says his wife is the apple of his life.

The paramedics were called to the home of an old couple. The man was not moving laying on the couch. The paramedics immediately went to work on him. The one said to the wife "I am sorry, but we can't find any life in him." The wife said "thats okay honey, I haven't found any life in him the last ten years".

The counselor gave the couple the usual assignment to write a list of what they liked and disliked about each other. He knew there was going to be a problem when the wife had a post note of what she liked and a large sheet of paper of what she didn't like.

The Royal couple was having a fight. Finally she reminds him of who wears the crown in the family.

The bee keeper calls his wife "Honey."
The astronomer calls his wife "My bright and morning star."
The weather man call his wife "Sunshine."
The baker calls his wife "Sweetie Pie."
The man who didn't have much until he married a rich lady calls his wife my "Goldmine."

Miscellaneous

Someone punched a fireman in his arm. He said be careful that is my firearm.

When a weather man doesn't know the answer he says he doesn't have the foggiest idea.

What do pregnant women and boys who hate school have in common? morning sickness

A lady who raises chickens says when she gets older that she is no spring chicken. She is more like a old brooding hen.

A skydiver likes to be the first one to jump and get the jump on the others.

A guy's nickname is weasel. I asked if that is because he tries to get out of things. He said no it was because he pops up everywhere.

A local radio station was broadcasting from the cemetery at night. They said they were the graveyard shift.

A psychic says "Don't be playing mind games with me."

A cleaner who has a drinking problem, we say she has been polishing off another bottle.

A miner says things may look good on the surface but we never know the problems that are underneath.

A word that can help you when opening gifts at Christmas is the word "different." When you don't like a gift or don't know what to say about it you say

"Well now isn't this different? What you are really thinking is I sure hope I can exchange this and get some money back.

Selling sheets for Halloween so people can be ghosts. The sign says one size fits all.

Some people are only smart around some people. They will tell them not to get smart with them.

You don't want this discussion with a skydiver on how high they can jump.

You don't risk having a bad hair day when you don't have any hair.

A guy in jail said he wished he was an artist. When asked what kind, he said an escape artist.

Some counselors make their living helping people who have experienced grief in their lives. This is where the expression "Good Grief" comes from.

Beauty operator tells lady she needs to take her hair to the cemetery. She said you have dead ends.

In Hawaii when you don't know what to say just say "Aloha."

At Halloween the truck isn't just a truck. It's a monster truck.

A man who worked with bees and honey had the nickname "Sticky fingers."

An electrician who has a bad temper is said to have short fuse. He is also the first to say he got the shock of his life.

When a race car driver has to go to the bathroom we say he is making a pit stop.

A man who was named "Robin" came from the Bird family. They are always trying to get money to feather their nest egg.

People who like stars like to go to all star events.

Unless I move I will never get rid of my pigeons. They are homing pigeons.

The architect has no excuse for how something was built because he designed it that way.

Lazy workers went on a sit down strike.

It is hard to compliment a cleaner. When you say you like what they are wearing, they say "Oh this old rag."

When a rabbit is upset it is hopping mad.

A sign at the campground says "Please no entertaining the bears or inviting them to lunch."

In his obituary of the nature lover it said he liked to squirrel away his time.

When they play bridge one lady always wondered why she ended up having to play the dummy.

A basketball player started his own chain of donut shops. They are called "Dunken Donuts."

A pilot said when he gets things wrong or seems confused he can always blame it on jet lag.

The man from discount tires was asked why he was married so many time including twice to the same person. He said so they don't get tired of you, you have to rotate them.

A friend telling her friend about her problem and the friend says nothing. Could you at least say something. Friend says "Something."

A magician can't find hide or hare of where his rabbits went to.

A guy told his friend he was thinking about getting a new mattress. His friend said you need to sleep on it first.

I love the Dutch book "The Windmills of Your Mind."

A sheep farmer that gets embarrassed feels "sheepish."

An honest gambler lays all his cards on the table.

I wasn't going to get into the conflict my artist friend was having, but he drew me in.
When someone is drunk the sanitation workers say he is wasted. If a carpenter is drunk they say he is hammered.

A guy in his twenties thought he was quite cool with the ladies. His house was a mess. He was a slob when it came to cleaning. He decided to call a house cleaning service to clean his place. He found one that said they provided top-less cleaners. That's who he called. So right on time on Thursday the doorbell rang. He excitedly opened the door, only to find a husky man there with a vacuum. He said can I come in. He came in and took his shirt off. He said his sister couldn't come so she sent him instead.

The only thing I want to scale back on is the bathroom scale.

There are a lot of jokes about electricity. It seems to be the current wave.

You think the cleaner is thinking clean thoughts but you would be wrong. They are usually thinking cleaning thoughts especially about the mess you made.

When the neighbors don't feed the mice often they come to your house for food.

We treat our right hand better than our left hand. We say to the right hand "right on." This makes our left hand feel left out.

What do you call sausage in Poland? Polish sausage

In Greece don't expect to understand anything it is all Greek to you.

He knew she would be good in art when she told him she was a pickup artist.

An astronomer said if things are going good for you, you need to thank your lucky stars. When he disagrees with someone he is heard to say "And what planet are you from?"

You should see the sanitation worker's trash collection. The sanitation worker's hold a beauty contest. The winner is crowned Miss Dumpster. A sanitation worker said when you keep having the same problem over and over again it is called recycling.

Bees are well trained. When they go back to the hive it is always in a bee line. The bee keeper said he may not have an A team but he definitely has a bee team.

The magician struggled with his act. He had no illusion about it being good.

When too many people at the power company are trying to get power it is called power surge.

A man was hanging his head down. He said he had too much on his mind and it was pulling his head down.

Two raccoons took stuff out of garbage cans. They made out like bandits.

A man said he has stomach problems. If he doesn't eat his stomach grumbles and complains. A friend said he has to learn not to listen to his stomach complain.

An astronaut calls his home town his launching pad.

I finally live in harmony. That is Harmony a small town in Kansas.

A robber trained by a cleaner makes a clean getaway.

The best compliment a weather man can give someone is to say they are a force of nature.

In this rural area they have benefits for one thing or another all the time. People are good at attending. They buy their ticket and show up. One guy asked another guy who the benefit was for for. He said it was for Tom Sullivan. He asked what is wrong with him? He was told nothing it was just a benefit for his benefit.

When you can't contain your emotions anymore it may be time to go to the container store.

A man owned another man some money. They spent some time together doing different things. The other man asked the guy who owned him money where the money was. The man answered "You know I have been spending time with you and time is money."

Even on vacation the pest control worker has trouble relaxing. He always has his fly swatter along and is on the lookout for flies or mosquitoes. At night he looks under the bed at the motel for bed bugs.

An older man said he always thought that cross dressing was when he wore one brown sock with one black one.

When a plumber is working and the pipe is hot he says it is pipping hot.

A trucker has so many problems and illness he said he is ready for an overhaul.

Someone asked the artist how he got the drawing so good. He said it was a long drawn out process.

A man says he never backed away from a fight. He did say however that he ran away several times.

When there are lot of Poles together in a community they tend to Polarize the community.

An auditor is said not to be all there. They say he is missing a few numbers.

When it is time for a librarian to go we say she has checked out.

When a trucker is down and depressed it can only only mean one thing. He is carrying too heavy a load.

Glamour news
There she is Heidi Lamont being taken out of the store in handcuffs.
Do you see those earrings? They much have cost thousands.
Look she is still wearing that necklace her third husband gave her.
The outfit she is wearing does nothing for her. Those pants are so tight and with the weight she has gained I don't know how she could get into them.
Wow look at those shoes. I heard she had them made special and they cost over five grand.
But her hair, I think it is time to say goodbye to one hair dresser. She definitely needs to find someone new. What do you say Frank?
Well there you have it folks remember more breaking news as it happens.

A speller overwhelmed with so many words to spell becomes spell bound.

The worse insult an apple grower can say is that someone is rotten to the core.

When a man buys a suit and later another man buys the same suit, we say he is following suit.

A trucker said he doesn't know how many times people have told him to hit the road.

A sanitation worker said he could do the job it was right down his alley.

An alert went out at the pest control place. There had been several phone calls telling that a bug was going around. The pest control people are not very impressed when someone catches a bug. Please they only caught one.

A sanitation worker said when he picked up trash in the trailer park that was what is called trailer trash.

People are saying they don't have to get their loved ones gifts this year. You know the saying "It is the thought that counts." We will get back to you later to tell you how that works out.

The landscaper is coming down with something. They say he is turning green. He already has a green thumb.

A man was told he had a big head. It said it was because he had an expanding mind.

Runners can be quiet when they run out of things to say.

I ran into Santa Claus two weeks before Christmas at a local cafe. All I could say was "Ho ho ho." He said "Ho ho ho to you too." I asked how he was doing getting down those chimney's? He said his body just fit each one, but if they weren't cleaned he had bad allergies and he would end up sneezing and waking up the whole household.

When an older man is talking to several other older men and holding his arms far apart. You know he is telling a fish story of the one that got away.

There was bad turbulence on the airplane. Passengers were shaken up and scared. One started singing "Nearer My God to thee." This was not helpful to the rest of the passengers.

A man was so tired swimming he said he felt like a dog. I said because you were dong the dog paddle? He said no because he made so many laps he felt like a lap dog.

A pitcher can get quite violent. A pitcher says he is within striking distance.

The carpet layer said he was always good at his job. When he was young they used to say he could really cut a rug.

A batter into Shakespeare says to the ball "You art a most foul ball."

A man said he used to get so upset and angry. He lost a lot of weight because everyone told him to walk it off.

Sign says if you must sleep on it let it be on one of our mattresses.

The bomber was going to put a bomb in the police station. The bomb was in the suitcase he was carrying. He brought it into the station which was quite busy and without anyone noticing it, he left it there and went back to his car. He got into his car and was ready to drive away. His back door opened. An officer said I am glad I caught you before you took off I will just put your suitcase in the backseat.

The puzzle maker said if you work to put the pieces together you will get a clear picture.

A lady got her hair done in bangs. Her boyfriend said the hairdresser did a bang up job.

Some guys were out in the Gulf on a fishing trip. Frank leaned over too far and fell in. Ted yelled "Frank jumped in. He is going to be shark bait for us."

The big squeeze is the name a boy gives his boa constrictor.

For both the painter and carpenter women are putty in their hands.

A question asked a grocery store stocker. How are things stacking up?

An engineer feeling down
He feels like he is on the wrong track.
He is just chugging along in life.
He is running out of steam.
If he doesn't find the right switch he is in trouble.
He is on a one way track headed for a train wreck.

A fireman doesn't just have a drill, he calls it a fire drill.

In a post office museum there are large boards filled with checks. These are the checks that people were told were in the mail.

When a bowler gets depressed he says his life is in the gutter.

When an oil man gets a flood of emotions they call it a gusher because the feeling come gushing out.

Boy to dentist don't take out my sweet tooth.

Eskimos can get kind of mushy when it comes to their dogs.

A cleaner had a fight with another man. It was a mop fight, the cleaner saying he was going to mop up the floor with him. If he has a little spat it is called a dust off.

Computer people don't eat regular potato chips they eat computer chips.

When a computer nerd is upset they say he is hacked off.

A marksman says he hasn't been felling well. He has been off his mark lately.

The grouchy dwarf had bad teeth and needed lots of dental work. You would be grouchy too if you had to go the dentist that often.

It was hard driving on the one street because it was so full of rabbits. The street is called carrot drive.

Don't have a conflict with your hairdresser over split hairs.
Many famous stars are not satisfied being a star they want to be the sun too. Now we all know that too much exposure to the sun can ruin someone.

A guy had been swearing like a crazy man all over the place. Someone asked him if he was related to the sanitation worker. He said no, but why? You are spitting out garbage all over the place.

You can get the best boots at the cowboy shop. All their boot salespeople have been sent to boot camp.

A miner who is depressed we say he is down in the pits.

Some people can't read joke books because they aren't into heavy reading.

Two people are talking to each other on their cell phones in the same room. That is what we call a close call.

A golfer can be lazy when asked to do any work they always claim they have a handicap.

When a golfer comes to the end of his life we say he has finished his course.

The people cleaners don't like are those who make tracks.

A man was describing to his friend his dream boat. He went on and on describing every feature. Finally his friend said I would love to see it. Show it to me. His friend said I can't show you, you need to have the same dream.

A laundry worker said life resembles a laundry. When you get older you get a lot of wrinkles, it takes longer to press on and there are more things to wash out.

Eggs are like our mind we don't want to crack or we will have scrabble eggs and a scrabbled mind.

The mind reader on the ship kept picked me to read my mind. She was so accurate, you could say I was well read.

A weather man says his only friends are fair weathered. He doesn't even have someone to ride out a storm with. He wishes he had some friends to shoot the breeze with.
There were rats at the car wash. I asked the manager what was up with them. He said they wanted to be washed so that nobody would call them a dirty rat.

A lady on a boat ride says she has a sinking feeling.

Sometimes when you tell a joke it falls flat. That is because some people instead of having a laugh line just have a flat line.

An older laundry worker said he felt he was on his last cycle of life. He said he felt he had just one final spin left.

Two ballerinas were talking. The one said it makes her so nervous when the director is always sneaking up on them. The other one said don't worry about it she is just keeping us on our toes.

A carpenter was building a house for a fireman. The fireman asked him to build a firewall.

A lady was so upset with herself she wasn't speaking to herself.

When a boxer is getting married we say he is down for the count.

You know he is a problem drinker when he says to everything anyone says "I will drink to that."

The archeologist could be very stubborn. In any argument he had he would not cave in.

The one reindeer was so upset. It was Dasher. It was said that he made a mad Dash.

A railroad engineer has a drinking problem. There is just too much chug a chugging going on.

The animal that has a drinking problem is a skunk. They say drunk as a skunk. That might explain why skunks smell. They raise their tail to warn you to stay away.

Four guys were taking about where they were born. The first said he was a native of Texas and born in Houston. The second said he was born in Ohio. The third said he was born in Canada. The fourth said he was born in a hospital.

A man said his dog wasn't happy just to be any dog. He wanted to be the top dog.

A clock maker said his enemy said he was going to clean his clock.

You don't want to hear the barber say "oops."

The band was playing outdoors on a cold night. After a few numbers they stopped and many of them went over to a camp fire that others had started earlier. One person asked a band member if they were done. He said no we are just warming up.

What the photographer says in the dairy department of the store "cheese."

You don't have to ask a cheater "Do you copy?"

"I am glad I caught up with you." What a highway patrol man says to a speeder.

What a deaf mute girl says to a guy. "Read my lips."

A lady went to a beauty consultant a few days before a big family wedding asked what she could do to make her look beautiful. After looking her over the consultant suggested she wear a veil to the wedding.

When a poultry farmer likes someone he says he is a good egg.

The miner was asked to bring something home for the evening meal. Of course he worked in a salt mine.

Lots of men are wearing goatees. I asked one if he liked goats. He said yes and he was feisty like a goat and said you don't want to butt heads with him. He said it was better than liking sheep because they are baaad.

The corn farmer said when he goes back to work he likes to pick up where he left off.

When a dairy farmer deals with stores he likes to go half and half.

If a carpenter went into wrestling he would be called the "Hammer."

In Idaho they don't say he is a stud, but a spud. Idaho is the state with the most eyes.

A farmer said he has been sitting on the fence many times and from his experience it can be quite painful.

You can't give too many jobs to a big eater because he already has a full plate.

It is hard to get a retired general out of the military. At home his office is called command central.

When a fireman shoots a gun they call him a hot shot.

Two men were talking. The one said he could never lie. The other one said than you better not run for public office.

The linen clerk is getting sick, she is as white as a sheet.

A bum arguing says "I beg to differ."

A man was seeing a counselor. Due to having done so many drugs he said he had lots of blanks in his life. The counselor said he would help him fill in the blanks.

A fighter says just because you win a round it doesn't mean you have won the fight.

A cowboy lassoed another cowboy. That cowboy was fit to be tied.

A baker likes to wear her hair in a bun.

Sign at a party shop says go ahead and pop our balloons.

Man to woman says you are as pretty as a picture. It is too bad that I am not very good with a camera.

A banker has fainted. Someone says quick get some hundred dollar bills and wave them under his nose.

A seamstress in trouble says don't pin this on me.

A short lady was self conscious about her size. She said she hates it when her boss belittles her.

A fighter was always at odds with his opponent. I never knew it would get so bad that it would come to blows.

When an auctioneer is dying they say going, going, gone.

Don't you hate it when you have something today and it is right on the tip of your tongue and you end up swallowing it?

Sometimes an idea is like an egg. You just have to sit on it for awhile and see what hatches.

A guy said he felt like he was coming apart. He had upset so many people they all wanted a piece of him.

You don't want to lend a book to this person. bookkeeper

A guy called his friend and told him to come over. He said he felt miserable. Why should I come over his friend asked. He said because misery loves company.

A carpenter and eye doctor have the same conflict over saying "I saw" or "I see."

The apple grower said it is important to get to the core of the problem.

When a lumberman first uses the computer he always logs on.

When we tell a story it is a colorful story. When we tell the truth it is the plain truth.

A heavy drinker may be in poor health, but in good spirits.

A writer said he has quit writing books. Now he only writes notes.
A naturalist said the dirt in his front yard is natural.

Wine growers get their information through the grape vine.

If you don't want a high temperature than you have to learn not to get all hot and bothered.

A vegetable farmer likes to tell veggie tales.

Vacation plans offered at the penitentiary are escape trips.

A carpenter has reached his benchmark in his career.

When you give money out and wished you hadn't that is called misgiving.

A surfer said he had to ride a wave of criticism. He said if he had let it get to him he would have been wiped out. A surfer says he has quit surfing, now he only surfs the internet.

A man signed a contract. He was called back to sign it agin. He had first signed it John Hancock.

Someone asked the rug man if he hunted. He said haven't you ever seen my bear rug?

A gambler was looking at spread sheets showing the different areas he placed bets on. He said you know I think I may be spread too thin.

Relief for many older people is when they can make it to the bathroom in time.

People are told they need to be centered. Unfortunately most of them are just self-centered.

An electrician that doesn't have it all together we say he is short circuited.

The watchmaker says at the end of the day that things are winding down.

At the cat show they have the famous cat walk.

A man says to another man that he feels beat. The other man said you should you just lost a fight.

The manager at the chicken farm was in a fowl mood.

When a cleaner dies we say she is swept away.

The lady was so emotional. She cried about everything all the time. She was labeled the town crier.

A man said he could communicate with the dead. An older lady said she had known Tom Sullivan for years and he had trouble communicating with the living.

A man says don't talk to me in my left ear. My wife already gave me an earful this morning.

Some times with power company workers there can be a power play which usually results in gridlock.

A man said he came from Poland to live here about twenty years ago. He said his parents still live in Poland. He said you could say we are poles apart.

A young lady was hoping to get into the limelight. Her friend said she didn't think lime was a good color for her.

The prisoner was so important he wasn't just put in a cell but a padded cell.

If someone from the royal family flushes he toilet it is called a royal flush.

When a miner runs a mile it is called milestone.

A man says it is okay when he has gas because it is natural gas.

If you get a dove be sure to get at least two of them. You don't want them to be a lonesome dove.

A new best selling book for students is called "One Thousand Excuses." A great book so you don't have to come up with the same excuse twice.

A neighbor asked the man where he was going in such a hurry. He said he was in a rush to catch his bus. The neighbor said it just left. How many people do you know in life that have missed the bus?

Paul W. Tastad

A man toured the Carlsbad Caverns in New Mexico. The elevator wasn't working. It was 265 steps to the bottom. People flooded down the stairs not remembering they had to later get up the stairs. When the guide was asked if everyone made it out he said there was a 90% success rate of getting them out.

Two Indians were talking finally the one said okay we will do it your way you're the chief.

The groundskeeper was arrested, He wanted to know on what grounds.

I was a natural leader when it came to trouble. I was seen as the ring leader.

I sleep a lot, but it is not my fault. I have lots of decisions to make and people tell me to sleep on it.

On our trip to the beach we had to shell out so much money.

When a linen salesman has too much to drink, they say he is three sheets to the wind.

My friend couldn't just have a boat he had to have a show boat.

The wizard says "Can you sit for a spell?"

What is the only country that makes excuses for their language? Pardon my French

When your short you don't see the same things as others. On a trip while sightseeing I mostly saw the back of people's heads.

With all the tattoos that statement it is written all over your face has taken on a new meaning.

If I am going to be smothered let me be smothered in kisses.

106

Insurance man says he can insure lots of things but he can't insure your happiness.

An author accused someone of stealing a page out of his book.

I am afraid he didn't fly over the cuckoo nest but ended up in it.

A mild mannered guy quit his job and started to do some very wild things. He said he answered the call of the wild.

A basketball player in trouble with the law. We say he ran afoul of the law.

Some people identify with bugs. They make pests of themselves.

During intermission at a concert an older man with hearing problems told his wife he couldn't hear most of the concert.
A man overhearing him said "You were lucky."

A young girl says she was so close to her idol she was only a heartbeat away.

They are carrying this political correctness too far. In a line up a lady yells "Thats the man that stole a kiss from me."

I was standing by my car and a man came up to me and said I have a bald spot. I said do you mean my head or the tires?

A bird watcher always thinks he knows everything. I asked him how he could be sure about something. He would say a little bird told him.

Most people suffer a hearing problem. They have select hearing.

A sign at a day care center says "We make many changes every day."

A trucker tells another trucker to stay away from him. He says he is fully loaded.

When you eat with an archeologist they always tell you to dig in.

When a guy goes to the malt shop he always asks "What is shaking?"

It was a great day for the postman when his son earned his first letter.

When the weatherman gets more energy we say he gets his second wind.

An orchard grower with a drinking problem we say he has been hitting the sauce.

When a dishwasher saw a UFO his eyes became as big as saucers.

The actor really wasn't too good. He always had to be propped up.

The clock maker is able to do so many things. He says it went just like clock work.

The only thing a poker player wants to draw is a straight.

An eye doctor does a magic act. It is called an optical illusion.

At the dentist convention to get everything off to a good start they release laughing gas.

It is hard to be good player when someone knows all your plays.

Diamonds are not just a girl's best friend. The jeweler is kind of in love with them too.

I had a problem. I was in the go before I was ready or set.

What does the junk yard dealer drive? A clunker of course.

A dairy farmer said he was the first one to come up with the idea of a straw poll.

Someone who wears stretch pants when it comes to telling their weight often stretches the truth.

The main flowers at a cemetery is daises. Everyone is pushing up daisies.

The best compliment a reporter can be given is to be called a snoop.

A man says to another man that it is as plain as the nose on your face. Than after looking at him more closely, he says well maybe not that plain.

I figured out where Big Foot is from. It has to be Texas because everything in Texas is bigger.

A telephone operator said she was on the quiz show "What's my Line."

What they say to people with dentures. Get a grip.

Cook telling the dishwasher to get busy says it is time for you to shine.

What one mountain climber said to the other mountain climber. "I will race you to the top." Than they ask you to help get them down

Only in Scotland do they ask who is wearing the skirt in the family.

Remember the ground on top is the top soil.

A photographer said you could tell what pictures were his because his prints were on them.

Old shoes are comfortable and we don't like to throw them out. The same with an old chair. Well for many our stomachs are comfortable just the way it is. It is called the comfort zone on the body.

A obituary said the lady never met a stranger. Of course she didn't. Even as a little girl I am sure her mother said don't talk to strangers.

Men are cheap Their best friend is a dog, for a woman it is a diamond.

For men if you have hair are bald, or partly bald the great equalizer is a cap.

Two small guys were fighting. A guy was watching them instead of working. He said he liked to watch a small fight.

A lady who has to read everything is called a "Readaholic." When a man reads too much he is a bookie.

A shop in the summer when the air conditioner isn't working is called a sweat shop.

Guys playing poker would say "I am in." The one guy trying to top the others would say "I am all in."

When the carpenters are having a party they have so much fun, people say they are raising the roof.

A large man goes into a small room. The realtor says that his presence fills the room.

A young hispanic man went to a counselor. He said he was sure that he was switched at birth. The counselor said he had heard that many times before. Just because your personality is different or you don't look like your parents I can assure you they are your parents. Why do you think you were switched? Because I am hispanic and my parents are Asian.

An animal trainer had a pigeon trained to come and fly down and sit on a stool. Of course it is a stool pigeon.

Don't drink too much pickle juice if you don't want to get pickled.

Man to his pet parrot. Quit parroting me.

A painter says in times of trouble he can't paint a rosy picture.

When a weather's man's son makes a hit in the music business we say he is taking the music industry by storm.

Who says the famous words "going down" and when he says it you better listen. A submarine captain

A young man lacked confidence in himself. When asked if he had any brilliant ideas, he said no just ideas.

A cab driver is accused of taking people for a ride.

A stocker thought he was better than anyone else. He only wanted to stock the top shelves.

At a twenty-fifth high school reunion, one lady kept staring at this man like she was trying to remember who he was. He came over to her and introduced himself. He asked her if she could place him. She hesitated. He said, "Oh come on. Can you place me?" She finally said okay third place.

A favorite book written by the weatherman is called "Nobody knows for such which way the Wind is blowing." It is a suspense novel.

An actor playing a role in a play doesn't want someone to tell him he is out of character.

If you test drive a car and have an accident does that mean you failed the test?

Signs at a cemetery
Make this your last stop.
We love our permanent residents.
You can make all the noise you want our residents won't care.
You can leave, but your body stays with us.

If a fireman tells bad joke it is called a smoke bomb.

Two guys were arguing over an idea. The one says to the other one "Do you even know where I am coming from?" The other one says I don't know New York or maybe California.

A run down barber shop is called a clip joint.

A fireman got a smoking jacket for Christmas. He said it was one of the hotter items.

A seamstress said there are so many things in her life that she has had to cut out.

An older man complains he can't help it if he gains weight. He doesn't remember very well and often can't remember if he ate so he eats again.

When you get old the magic word that brings a smile to most senior citizens is the word "bingo."

The farmer said that every day he works he has a field day.

Your mind is like a camera. With it you take pictures. A guy said he must be out of film.

A man with a split personality was always arguing with himself.

A mouse found in a cleaning lady's house is squeaky clean.

A man buying glasses says he wants to look out through rose colored glasses.

When you make too many mistakes they send you to a corrections center.

People always talk about the cheese on the moon, but few remember the moon pies.

We all know why a dog was called Puddles.

A man was the guest speaker at the school for the hearing impaired. He said he was afraid his talk fell on deaf ears.

In China they don't have common flies they have dragon flies.

Man bought a ticket for a kiss at a kissing booth. When he got there the lady said she was sold out.

The pastor tells the bride to be that he knows that three of her past boyfriends will be at the wedding, but he still doesn't think it is appropriate to have the song "Who's sorry now."

Some people on a quiz show
The forest ranger was doing good until he got stumped.
The clock maker was doing good until he ran out of time.
The detective said he had proof that he was right.
The tow truck driver felt he could pull off a win.
The party girl when she lost felt like someone had popped her balloon..
A thief tried to steal the show.
A math teacher would have done okay if she hadn't miscalculated her opponent.
The race car driver would have been okay if he hadn't been in such a hurry.
The hunter said he was lucky he just took a shot in the dark and happened to be right.

A guy looked at another guy went over to him and spit on him. "Hey what is wrong with you, why did you do that?" He said there is a guy he can't stand and you are the spitting image of him.

Funeral director selling a casket says now this one he will probably be the most comfortable in.

If you want to feel power hold lots of keys. Everyone will have to come to you.

A man said he had so much stored in his brain. He was glad there was no charge for storage.

A rug guy when in trouble he is called on the carpet.

With the price of ammunition these days, no one is taking cheap shots at anyone.

A man goes into a confessional booth at a Catholic church and starts confessing. Here are some of the responses to what he says. "You got to be kidding. And nobody suspected what you were up to. I can't believe you got away with it. You are a bad man." Finally the man confessing asks "Father is that you?" The other guys says no the priest was called out earlier. He said he just came in because it was cold outside and decided to sit for awhile.

The name of the new beauty shop is "Cut and Dry."

The hardest thing about being stranded on a desert island by yourself, if you don't get along with yourself.

The weather man was in a fight. He gave the other guy gave him a cold cut to the chin. Than he knocked him out cold.

A fortune teller was with two young ladies telling the fortune to one of them. She said I see a great emptiness in your life. Her friend said are you sure you don't mean her mind?

A carpenter rode off on his sawhorse leaving saw dust behind him.

How people get out of things when someone is talking to them. They look at the clock and say "oops I got to run."

Sign says let us help you with your bills. We will consolidate all your bills and you will make just one huge payment to us.

In a rural county a girl was crowed Miss Dairy Princess. A guy whispered to a friend you should see her mother she is a real cow.

Sometimes when an artist is pushed too far they will just draw a line.

When the Volkswagen beetle was being sold people were encouraged to catch the bug fever.

Santa was the original person who was on top of things. He worked so hard he went to see a lawyer because he needed to have some time off. The lawyer was able to get Santa a clause.

A polite beggar says "I beg your pardon."

I was upset with my neighbor. I called him up and said come over and get your mouse that is in our garage.

At the grocery store I saw a girl who had dyed her hair bright red. The only thing I could say to her was "Hey Red."

There are lots of professors in the mental hospital. They are called the "Nutty professors."

The name of the boxing school is called the "School of hard knocks."

An artist was drawing and a friend looked at the drawing and asked what it meant. The artist said you have to draw your own conclusions.

When a cleaner dies we say she is swept away.

An electrician may get kind of wild when he is over charged.

I agree with the electrician sometimes the news is quite shocking.

There was going to be a painting workshop. Everyone was asked to send in a picture of something they had painted. The staff would look over the pictures and decide who to invite to the workshop. One staff member looking over the pictures showed it to a coworker. It was picture of a wall that the person had painted.

The movers moved the table but lost the legs to the table. They said the table doesn't have a leg to stand on.

A poster in a dental office shows a man sitting alone in a waiting room while a lot of people are crowded on the other side of the room. It is a lonely world for a man with bad breath.

A pilot does not have an attitude problem but an altitude problem. He thinks he is above everyone else.

There is a fitness program at the county jail. It is to get them fit enough to stand trial.

I know a guy that is so smart they have a brain trust started for him.

They were going to let one of the new team go but the boss wanted it to remain a secret. But than the weatherman got wind of it.

A writer upset with someone is said to have written them off.

The apple growers are the first ones to say about their children "The apple doesn't fall far from the tree."

He seems a little off. Oddly enough he works at the mental hospital.

The baker's daughter is called their flour child.

Daylight saving time ended. A worker at a club was told to change the six clocks. He moved them into different positions.

A painter says to another painter that he found the perfect place to hang his pictures. It is in the school for the blind.

What you do may not be insane, but it definitely borders on insanity.

At the cemetery they like the families to stay together. That is why they offer a family plot.

A dairy farmer was having trouble. He had been selling skim milk instead of whole milk and skimming off the profits.

A dairy farmer seldom reads the whole book. He just reads the condensed version.

My cleaning lady likes to talk mess with me.
She has helped me get out of many a sticky situation.
She knows where to find the dirt.
She also knows the dirt on everyone.
She says she lives a clean life.
Nobody is going to find any dirt on her.

Because of his name lots of people do things for hm. His name is Pete you know for Pete's sake.

When an astronomer goes on vacation he likes to stay at a five star hotel.

A girl was asked how she got the nickname "Ida." She said when she was little she was asked who did it and she would say "I did a".

A guy from a medium sized city always bragged what a big giver his Grandfather was. He gave the most when they built a new church, and for the new library. You name it he was the biggest giver by far. Finally one day someone challenged him. He said I looked up all the records when you say your Grand father gave and his name is not mentioned. Well he says my Grandfather was a humble man and when he gave it was always anonymous.

We know the first robin is a sign of spring, but there is another sign given by the birds. It is those love birds.

What person do most people think needs glasses? An umpire at a baseball game.

Nickname for junkyard man is scrappy.

When you get older, absence has nothing to do with the heart but the mind. You have trouble remembering who they are.

They now have happy hour for the cars. At one oil changing place it says get your oil changed from three to four you will get half off.

The weather man sees the news as earth shaking. The weather man is not a good runner. He always gets winded. The weather man likes to read chilling novels that send a chill down his spine. He never says "Don't leave me out." but "Don't freeze me out."

When a book lover dies it is the last chapter of their life.

When a subway conductor dies they say it is the end of the line.

The dancer said he learned all his moves when working for a moving company.

A game the sanitation workers like is " Go to the Dump."

A turkey was gobbling so much. The turkey farmer got tired of hearing it and said he was going to stuff it.
The artist was drawing the face of a man and it got a little long. Someone asked her why the long face?

When Fred died his family had him cremated. When the sons left after the funeral to go eat one of them panicked. He said I laid Fred down and now I can't find him anywhere. It is hard to lose your dad twice in such a short time.

Life wasn't easy for a swimmer. Most of his life he had to swim against the current and upstream.

Who was named by a baby? Try Ga Ga Lady Ga Ga

A vampire had been acting so negative. I asked him what was wrong. He said he had been drinking too much negative blood.

When someone says they have seen a ghost we say they have been spooked.

A guy was late going to a meeting. He said he was stopped by a highway patrol man while going just a little over the speed limit. He told the patrol man that lots of cars were speeding and going faster than he was. He asked why he was the one picked up. The officer said you were the easiest one to catch.

The window man's bad news is glass shattering.

The weatherman's news is ice breaking.

Matt has such wonderful curly hair. His nickname was Curly. Now many years have passed and so has his hair. Now the only things he can curl is his toes.

A sign at a cemetery says this is the place where your loved ones will finally find the rest they need. Another sign says when you leave we get to keep your body.

When a former football player is at the end of his life we say he is in his end zone. It can be a difficult time to climb the ladder of success when someone takes the ladder.

It was said that the librarian speaks volumes.

When a landscaper gets tired we can say that he is bushed.

A forest ranger that gets off course we say he has lost his path and he is way off the trail.

When we get older and talk about runs we are not talking about baseball but runs to the bathroom.

A man said he is such a deep thinker that sometimes he can't get his thoughts to the surface.

People who believe in ghosts say that even if you bury your problems later they will come back to haunt you.

A skydiver and his friends had a falling out.

Baseball players who have a drinking problem we say they have been hitting the bottle.

What the unhappy mother of the bride said to her concerning the groom. "You can do better."

Most people need help with good excuses. Most of the time they just use the standard excuses.

It is not easy to understand stock broker's jokes. They are mostly insider jokes.

You don't want to get on the wrong side of a photographer. They can make you look bad.

A bad egg is called a deviled egg.

A teenage girl while driving out of the parking lot at a mall ran into another car.

The driver of the other car got out, and she recognized him as the neighbor who lives down the street. She said to him "Imagine running into you here."

The policeman stopped a lady who went through a red light. He asked her if she hadn't seen the light. She said "My day has been so bad. We all overslept and the kids missed the bus. I had to get their lunch ready. We were late for everything. In all the confusion I left my glasses at home. I can' t see much of anything without them."

In the days of the caveman there were lots of stones and rocks. It was soon discovered that their children picked out special ones. These were their precious stones.

A boy was yelling at a grocery store. The clerk said it was the parent's fault. The parent told him to yell if he needed anything.

To get information from terrorists they used all sorts of torture. Not anymore. They are sending them to the dentist who will work on them without using any novocain. I can just hear the dentist say "Do you want to talk or do I need to drill a little deeper?

Movies/Music

The movie "A River Runs Through It" is about a great flood and of course it ran through the middle of the house.

The movie "From Riches to Rags" is about a stockbroker who made poor investment choices.

There is a movie called "I Married an Axe Murderer." In the movie the star talks to his best friend. His best friend tells him to remember nobody is perfect, his wife probably just has an axe to grind. At the end it is so touching when he and his wife go into the back yard and bury the hatchet.

The movie "The Big Chill" is about a weatherman going to a family gathering on his wife's side of the family.

The movie about the parole system is called, "Catch and Release."

The movie "The two faces of Eve" is about before and after her face lift.

A horror film was a great hit. There was so much screaming in it. Halfway through the film mice would be released into a screaming audience with many of them running out.

The movie "Look who is talking" has been out for years. Now twenty years late they did a remake of the movie called "Look who won't shut up."

The movie was about a group of friends having a party. Soon the party took a dark turn. What happened was that the electricity went out.

New movie by some air conditioner guys is called "Be Cool."

The movie "The Quick and the Dead" is about those who are quick on the draw and of course, if they aren't they are dead.

There is a remake of the movie "Oliver Twist." The new movie has a new twist in it.

The movie "A Dirty Weekend" is about parents of two college age kids who after being home for the summer go back to college leaving the parents to clean their rooms.

The movie "All is Lost" is about a gambler that lost everything including the house.

The movie "Field of Dreams" is about a farmer who was caught by his wife out in the field sleeping instead of working.

The movie is about a long road trip. It has a very scary ending. When it comes to the end it says dead end.

The movie "From Rags to Riches" is about a cleaner who married her rich boss.

The movie "No Man's Land" means the land belongs to the government.

A new scary movie in Egypt is called "The Mummy Returns." If your mummy had died and than come back you would be scared too.

At intermission of a play one actor said to another actor "Don't you love the roar of the crowd?" The other actor says "It sounds more like their booing to me."

The movie "The Lady and the Tramp" is so unfair to men. She is a lady and he is a tramp. I bet you couldn't get by reversing the roles.

The movie "In the Heat of the Night" is about being in the middle of the night and the furnace kicks in.

The first movie was titled the bad. The second the very bad. The third the very very bad. Finally they came out with the movie "The Superbad."

There is a movie out called "Nobody Walks." Of course the movie is about the cab drivers in New York City where everyone rides.

They are remaking the movie "Total Recall." It is now titled "I Can't Recall." It is especially a hit with the older people.

Shame on the people who made the movie "The Shaggy Dog." With all the grooming facilities it should have been groomed.
A movie for carpenters is called "Down the Sawdust road."

In band a student was supposed to play the chimes. He forgot when to play them. The band conducted said "You can chime in anytime."

A music teacher is off his rhythm. He is now singing the blues.

If a basketball player is into music just bounces along.

When the fruit growers get together for music they call it a jam session.

A piano player said to a singer "I don't believe there is a key for what you are singing.

Eye doctors songs
When I have double vision I get to see twice as much of you.
I have my Eye on you.
I hope I don't have to get crosseyed with you.

A singer and a baseball player are both hoping to have a big hit.

Old Geezers singing group
Slow down your going too fast.
Get out of my rocking chair.
Bring back our Yesterdays.
There is no fool like an old fool.
I have got you on my mind, now if I could just remember who you are.

The song from those who finished the twelve step program
How dry I am.

Dishwasher song
When I think of you I get all soapy.
I get all emotional thinking of our good times and get suds in my eyes.

A song by former astronauts is called "Fly me to the Moon."

Farmers favorite dance is the barn dance.

A man who is good at music and baseball is said to have a perfect pitch.
Calendar girls sing
Their first song of course was Monday Monday.
Your days are numbered.
We have yet to set a date for you.
Their new hit is "I am going to clear my calendar and make a date for us."

Writer's singing group
Signature song
Some sing under a pen name
Don't cramp my style
I don't want to have to say the hard word
It will be over when the last word is written
Words can only express how I feel about you.

Songs "Standing on the Corner" "Thumbing a ride" and "I want to go with you" these are all pick me songs.

A man's wife had a small solo part in the Christmas program. After she sang he said to his friend "Doesn't she sing like an angel?" A man two rows in back of him said ''She sings like a fallen Angel. That is not any heavenly music."

Money Song
Where has all the money gone?

Where has all the money gone?
Gone to bills everywhere.
Gone to bills everywhere.
When will it ever return?
Only when I win the lottery or probably never.

A music director told the group singing that the sound is off.

The Demolition singers broke up for awhile. Than they tried to pick up the pieces and get back together.

A music group is called the movers. The problem is to find them because they are always on the move.

Songs from the new music group called "The mighty mice."
It is a Rat race out there.
You got cheese, I got cheese everyone got cheese.
Big Bad Kitty
Don't Hole up on me
When they are through everyone screams and squeals.

Demolition boys singing group
One word best describes their singing it is dynamite.
They are having a blast when they sing.
It will knock your socks off.
Than there is an explosion.
After that they bring the house down.

When the music teachers leaves someone she always says "Now stay in tune."

The music teacher told her student to read her notes, and not to be skipping any notes.

Someone asked what I sang. I said off-key.

Music instructor to student you need to be on my beat.

The sanitation workers have a new music group called the "Backyard Boys." Some of their songs are "Something smells," "Don't bring up yesterday's garbage," and "Our love can be recycled" and "I can only hope I don't have to dump you."

A man in prison finally got a big break. Well maybe not the biggest because that would be to break out. He made a recording. Some of the songs are: "Release me," "Oh Judge Oh judge won't you pardon me," "I am doing time with you on my mind," and "I am not conning you when I say I love you, but I do want to steal your heart," and "If you would only bail me out me we could spend more time together. Their last song is when he escapes called "On the Run again." With these songs there will definitely be some jail house rock.

The door men have a new group made up of guys who actually work on doors. Some of their songs are "You can knock but you can't come in," "Knock knock don't come knocking on my door," "Knock three time if you want me to come out," "Don't slam the door on our relationship," " I feel like a revolving door when you come and go," and "Baby I am afraid I have to end my open door policy".

A choir director tells student trying out for choir, I don't like the tone of your voice.

A music group of sheep shearers is called the Wooly Boys.

Some claim they hear a haunting melody at the old opera house.

Her voice was so high, we had to talk her into coming down.

I know she is a good singer, but does she have to be so vocal about it?

The song "California Dreaming" was started by some snow bound people in Minnesota.

The bass singer sang the note so low he brought the song to a new low.

The director says some students don't take direction very well.

Musician knows when he is good. He feels those good vibrations.

Songs by the morticians
Blast from the Past
Don't walk on my Grave
We will help you bury your problems
Don't be a stiff, but come and Party with us

Songs of the cleaners
Ragtime blues
I am all spit and polish
I will clean up for you
Don't just mop around
Your fingerprints need to be found in my house.

Songs of the fireman
Baby light my fire
My eyes get all smoky when I think of you
Don't quench the burning fire we have together
I am sending you smoke signals that say I love you
We need to fan the flames of our love

In France a little by was a bed wetter. The mother asked the father to check if he had wet the bed. The father comes back singing the song "A la wet a a la wet a." They now sing this all over France.

A music teacher said her husband would tune her out. He said you can't live the rest of your life on a high note.

Years ago Elvis"s Mother and Aunt were in a car accident. Elvis not being around them called and asked how they were. The aunt said she was shook up. His mother said she was all shook up. Elvis said say that again. Now you know the story how the song "I am all shook up" came into being.

The choir director turns around and puts cotton in his ears. He than tells the student it is okay for her to hit that high note again.

Years ago this music was the music for cleaners. It was the Ragtime blues.

When a music teacher's boyfriend finally asked her to marry him, she said it was like music to her ears.

There were problems in the choir. There were chords of discontent. The choir teacher told the bass singer that he was way off base.

A song from a group of weathermen is titled "My Sunshine will Blow your Clouds away."

To be a success in music you have to move your lips and your hips.

When a gardener goes tho a music festive he calls it a hoedown.

The music teacher asked the student if he could sing a few bars. The student sings bar bar bar.

He didn't sing well with others because he always wanted to be the lead singer.

A miner likes music that rocks.

A choir director goes over his day verse by verse.

The plumbers have a musical group songs are:
"Don't flush our love down the toilet."
"You rattle my pipes."

"I get all clogged up when I talk to you."

"I am afraid I will have to pull the plug on our relationship."

"Don't yank my chain."

Than there is the plumbers lament. They sing when they are down and depressed all they can sing is "Drip, drip and drip."

When they know there is something wrong with a relationship there new hit is "Something smells here."

These songs are going fast. You need to get them before they got down the drain.

A song for procrastinators is "Tomorrow" "I will do it tomorrow, please don't asked me to do it again today."

Seamstress songs "Don't tear us apart." "We weren't cut out for each other." "Let's just patch things up and we can be sewed back together, and I am on needles and pins while I wait for you."

The band was so loud someone said they could raise the dead. Another commented that he hoped they didn't play in a cemetery.

Relationships

When you went out with someone you didn't know too well, but your friend wanted you to go out with her and the date was just okay. When they ask you how it went you can always say "It was something."

A hunter said his girlfriend moved out of range. A hunter said he had lots of dates. He told them he came fully loaded.

Girl friend of race car driver tells him that true love can't be rushed.

The watch maker changes boyfriends so often they are called the man of the hour.

A girl was engaged to a miner. She called him her rock, but told him when they got married she wanted to see a bigger stone on her finger.

It is love for a vampire at first bite.

A baseball player says that when a girl has no boyfriend that means she is in play.

A seamstress said she was torn apart trying to decide between two different men.

A girl asked the guy if he wanted to tango. He asked why. She said it takes two to tango.

A girl had been dating a runner. They had a fight. Her last words to him had been " Don't run off now."

A man liked dating the operator. She would always keep an open line for him and she had lots of connections.

A sanitation worker said he found love at the curb. A boyfriend threw his girl-friend to the curb. It was just in time for the worker to pick her up. He also promised to drive her around the neighborhood and they could see what the neighbors are putting out.

An operator broke up with a man because she didn't like his number. She had so many other dates she assigned them unlisted numbers.

A gambler to another gambler says "If you play your cards right you could win her heart."

A girl was dating a electrician. He came over to her parent's house and talked nonstop and was all over the place. When he left she said to her parents he sure is a live wire. The father said "And you know what they say about live wires is don't touch them."

I saw this guy as a window of opportunity.
What I saw I liked. Unfortunately the window wasn't too clean.
He was such a paine.
We had to open the window to air our grievances.
He was so blind to his behavior.
I was hoping to find shade from the sun, but instead he let the sun in.
I am going to shut the window on this part of my life.
I just shutter thinking what my life with him might have been.

A baseball player said he couldn't get a date and was afraid if he asked too many girls and got turned down he would be out of the game. He went to another player and I do mean player here. He taught him how to be a hit with the girls and even get dates with some being out of the ballpark.

A girl was dating this guy who had a little too much weight in his stomach. She liked him, but couldn't get him to exercise.

I said there was only thing she could do. When you went out with him she was clumsy and kept dropping things so he would have to bend over the pick them up.

My son works at the zoo. He went ape over a girl that worked there. She messed up so many times but he stuck his neck out like a giraffe for her. When he was with her he was proud as a peacock.

A girl said her boyfriend was like a rooster. He was always strutting his stuff and crowing about what he did. He was just too cocky.

A water man said his feelings in the relationship go from hot to cold.

When asked about his date he said he wasn't impressed he was under-impressed.

A plumber says that sometimes his feelings and emotions are just like the toilet they overflow.

A banker said his girlfriend tries to get too much from him. She is definitely overdrawn.

A math teacher said her boyfriend was a little off. He was definitely an odd number.

A fireman said he had a flaming passion for a certain lady. Now he said his fire is 90% contained.

A dishwasher was getting ready for a date. He said," I have to wash up first. This is my night to shine. I won't be in hot water all night. I know my boss gave me a hard time, but I can dish it back as well as the next guy".

A dairy farmer said the girl he is in love with just melts his butter.

Girl calls her boyfriend and tells him how bored she is at her job. She asks him what he is doing. He says that everything is dead around here. She says to her girlfriend "He works at a funeral home."

I asked a girl why she wore such bright clothes. She said she wanted her boyfriend to think she was bright.

A guy thinks his girlfriend loves herself too much. She looks in the mirror and says "I love you" and than kisses the mirror.

A worker for the waste department said his last relationship was toxic.

An investor said he is not good at long term relationships unless he can see some benefits early on.

An orange grower said he has had several girlfriends, but the one he really likes is his main squeeze.

A cowboy was excited to find a girl that liked to go horseback riding with him. She had never been on a horse before. For months they rode together almost everyday. He was hoping she was growing closer to him, but instead she fell in love with the horse and rode off and left him.

A boy in love kept whispering in a girl's ear. She said why do you keep saying "nothing, nothing" in my ear. He said they were sweet nothings.

A girl was so popular guys were lined up to take her out. Suddenly John was no longer one of them. He had got out of line.

A guy said his date ate so many lemons when they went out that she became sour halfway through the date.

A baseball player was no good asking girls out. He had to get a pitch hitter.

A young man tells the young lady working at the library he wants to check her out. He says they are over due for a date. She says she checked on the last book he read. It was "How to Win over Girls and Easily Influence Them." She tells him that if he tries that with her she will fine him.

Guy to girlfriend tells her she is his universe.
Girl says back than your world is too small.

The dry cleaner's boyfriend was so clingy. She wanted the relationship to be cling free.

A girl is starting to like a weather man. She is warming up to his ideas.

A basketball player picked up with an old girlfriend. He said he got her on the rebound.

Boy to girlfriend. "Words cannot express how I feel about you." She says well maybe you should try money.

Cleaner to boyfriend don't start a mess with me.

A parking meter lady was in love with a man. She told him he had better know where to park his car and that would be in her driveway. She said I am getting older and my meter is running.

A friend asked her girlfriend why she still liked her boyfriend who was in prison. The girl answered that are lots of advantages. I always know where he is. He isn't stepping out on me. He doesn't have any other girls around him. He is looking good pumping all the iron and he has plenty of time to write me letters.

A young guy said his girlfriend is so special. When she is in the crosswalk, all traffic stops for her.

The eye doctor told his girlfriend to remember that he was going to keep an eye on her. His other girl friend was so much trouble he said she was a real eye opener for him.

A pilot was on a flight with his girlfriend who was the stewardess. They were having an argument. He said we are landing soon and I hate to keep this up in the air.

Man says to girlfriend I know you are priceless. That is why I no longer can afford to have you for my girlfriend.

A postman said his girlfriend is close to him. They both live in the same zip code.

An English teacher said her boyfriend talks and talks and doesn't know how to use a period.

A bread man broke up with his girlfriend. He said all that is left of their relationship is crumbs.

It is hard dating someone from the lighting company. They always want the spotlight on them.

An astronomer knows he is in love when his girlfriend sees stars in her eyes.

A weather man is now advising couples who are going to get married.
He gives them his forecast.
For some he sees sunny days ahead.
Others he sees that they are in for a stormy time.
Some he sees a cloud on the horizon.
Some he warns of ice patches ahead.
He encourages others to wait until the sky is clear.
Many are in a fog and can't really see where their relationship is going.

A sailor came home on leave and found his girlfriend had a new boyfriend. She told him to sail on.

It rained a week before the wedding of the weatherman's daughter. He told her he had promised her a shower.

A photographer asked a girl he liked if she could picture the two of them at a park near a waterfall while he was holding her hand. She said she could picture the waterfall and the park, but couldn't see him in the picture.

Girlfriend of skydiver said he hasn't been dropping in like he used to.

A gal around twenty-eight was having a hard time finding a man to be in her life. Most of her friends were married or going out with someone. including most of her coworkers, but nobody seemed to notice her enough to ask her out. Finally she came to me for help. First thing she had was a make over and learning how to use makeup. Than her hair was done over. Than she had to learn to wear clothes that made people look at her. She had a picture of a gorgeous male model on her desk and she told everyone that was her new boyfriend. Everyday there would be flowers, little gifts and of course lots of phone calls. Everyone got so jealous and the guys started to pay attention to her. Finally after a month he showed up to talk to her and of course everyone listened in. He said how much fun she was and he loved being with her. Unfortunately he had decided to was going to try to get back together with his wife. After he left all those listening had tears in their eyes. After that many wanted to comfort her and of course a number of guys were ready to ask her out.

It was hard for Frankenstein to get many dates. Girls were always saying that he creeped them out.

One lady CIA operative said to another CIA lady operative who had her eyes on a certain guy, don't get any ideas I spied him first.

The security man said when he met his daughter's boyfriend he knew something was wrong. His alarms were going off all over.

Girl to her girlfriend says "I know you think I stole Jack from you, but I was just trying to keep you from making a mistake.

Cab drivers can be so romantic. They always like to remember at what intersection they first meet their girl.

The electrician told his daughter's ex-boyfriend he didn't want him to darken their door again.

If a landscaper is in love we say it is a budding romance.

A lady mechanic says her boyfriend gets her engine running.

A waitress in love with the cook said she wanted him to see her as the main dish instead of just another side dish.

Forest ranger in love
He says he pines for her.
He hopes their paths can cross more often.
He says she should follow his trail
He says for her to tell her old boyfriend to take a hike.
Go out with me and we can be trail blazers.

An unromantic fellow at a movie with his girlfriend. She says she is cold. He gives her his sweater, instead of his arm.

A guy knew his friend either went out with girls that were either beautiful or had lots of brains. He hadn't meet the latest girlfriend. He finally went to a party and someone pointed out who the girlfriend was. He looked her over and over. He thought she must really be smart.

A girl went out with a rich fireman. He said he had money to burn.

At first I didn't get anywhere with the librarian. Finally she agreed to give me a second reading.

When the weather man saw her standing out in the rain, not knowing enough to get out of the rain. I knew she was the girl for me. She needed someone to take care of her.

An archeologist is not the best candidate to marry. A girl said she didn't like his digs. She also didn't want to dwell in a cave with him.

At camp I hurt my ankle. A kind guy carried me back to camp. I knew he was the right one for me. You could say I got carried away.

If you are looking for lost causes you don't have to look much further than my last boyfriend.

A fortune teller said I was going to meet a tall, dark and handsome man and sure enough I did. Later he introduced me to his very sick and very rich father. Guess which one I married.

A trucker said he met a gal who told him to sit down and take a load off.

Postmaster tells girlfriend he will seal it with a kiss.

Some guys were talking. One said the one guy was a chick magnet. The other guy asked if he worked on a chicken farm.

Girlfriend of postal worker tells him to be sure and keep her posted.

A girl said her boyfriend is into nature. He is always hugging a tree. I want to tell him that I have limbs too and I could use a hug.

The boy is so cheap he will only date girls from the Netherlands. They go Dutch when they go out.

It is good dating an elevator operator. He always lifts you up.

A runner got rid of his girlfriend's last boyfriend. He ran him off.

A young lady says she has so many things she wants to get plugged into. The problem is that her boyfriend doesn't have any connections.

An eye doctor said he was first attracted to this lady that caught his eye. I asked what happened. He said they later lost eye contact.

You know you are in trouble with your date when it is just dusk out and he says let's call it a day.

A girl says she is trying so hard to be sweet. She knows you catch more flies with honey, but than who wants flies when your trying to catch a boyfriend.

You can tell her boyfriend is a baseball player by the way he bats his eyes.

A guy likes to call girls his cousins. His friend says that just because he wants them to be his kissing cousins.

A painter finally found the right guy. She said he just needs a little touch up here and there.

In going out with a gambler you have to know when to hold him and when to fold and leave him.

A mover was proud of his coworker. He never had to hook him up with a date. When he found the right one they got married without a hitch.

A shoe salesman and his girlfriend broke up. They were not on equal footing.

A man was trying to date an telephone operator but she kept giving him a busy signal.

A mechanic said his girlfriend's romantic name for him is you big lug nut.

A man who worked for the oil company told his girlfriend who worked for the gas company that they needed to break up. He said oil and gas don't mix.

It was a hard race but he gave it all he had. He came in fourth. He knew he couldn't date the girl he wanted to impress. She said earlier she only dates winners.

A friend calls his girlfriend "Sugar." His friend says she is too sweet for you.

A guy went out with his girlfriend whom he called "Sunshine." He says he was with her so much he suffered sunburn.

When a mild manner man goes out with a spicy girl there is bound to be some flare-ups.

An operator is in a relationship with a long distance runner. She told her boyfriend if he liked her so much to give her a ring.

My boyfriend was on his hands and knees when I went to his house. I thought he was going to propose. Instead I found out he was washing the floor.

I liked it when I dated a girl named Blessings. Her father would say "You have my Blessings."

When a teenage boy's shoulder is all wet you can bet his girlfriend has been crying on it.

A gas station worker has been trying to get his girlfriend to go back with him but had no success. He doesn't know what more to say. He says he is running on empty.

A street guy would wait outside this fancy apartment building every day and talk to this beautiful lady when she came home from work. To live there you know she had money, and was beautiful and seemed to be smart. The street man had no job, or money, and wasn't too good looking. He finally got up the courage one day to ask her to go out with him. She said why should I go out with you. He said you know opposites attract.

The girl was nearing thirty. All her friends were married and having children. A friend asked her what happened that she was still single. She said she was told to play hard to get and maybe she played too hard to get.

A cook was upset with his girlfriend. He said she was acting like spoiled food that needed to be thrown out.

How different people got together.
A gambler said it was just luck.
A golfer said it was a stroke of luck.
A coast guard man said he had to rescue her because she was adrift.
A librarian said she just had to check you out.
An executive said it was a power play when he won you over.
A salesman said he had to sell you on the idea.
A baseball player said he had to work to catch you.

My girlfriend likes to run every morning. She has got another thing coming if she thinks I am going to run after her.

An air conditioner guy says if you go out with him you can learn to be cool in every situation.

A girl says not only is the public not interested in her E-mails she can't even get her boyfriend to read most of them.

Spiderman went out with this lady that was a great cook. He would eat and say to her that was amazing. She said you are amazing too. The name stuck. To this day Spiderman is called " Amazing Spiderman".

The operator at the merry go round asked a girl if she wanted to go another round with him.

Everyone including a young lady named Hope were outside. One boy was holding Hope. He said he was holding onto Hope.

A man came into the club and kissed a lady. When asked who she was he said it was his wife. Another guy asked who was that lady you kissed yesterday at the club.

When the romance is going out for a fireman sometimes he just needs to fan the flames.

A fisherman who is trying to pick up girls keeps throwing out the wrong lines. His lines tend to be sinkers

A computer nerd says his girlfriend really likes him. She downloads everything he says.

It was predicted in high school that she would marry someone rich. Sure enough later in life you married Rich Klein.

A baseball player was having trouble in asking girls out, he said his game was off.

A girl was out eating on a first date with a boring man. She said that when she is with him time stands still. She thought to herself "I sure wish is would hurry up so I can get this date over with."

The dishwasher's girlfriend is called his main dish. He broke up with another girl earlier who was one hot dish. He said as soon as he was out of hot water and dried off he was ready to go with her.

There is a problem with dating when you are older. At a party this lady comes and talks to you and mentions the good times you had together several years ago and you keep thinking to yourself "If I could just remember who she is."

The trapeze artist was flying high when he caught the girl of his dreams.

In high school this guy was quite an attraction for the girls. They didn't like that his eyes were blue, brown or green. He had dreamy eyes. Some would daydream about him at school and others would dream about him at night. They called him "Mr. Sandman."

Sports

A hunter kept shooting off his mouth. He acted like he knew everything and was always telling others what to do. He suddenly got kind of quiet. His companion asked him what was up. He said he ran out of shells.

A hunter said at target practice he was the best shot of his friends. The friends decided to go on a hunting trip. He said he didn't know what to do. He loved animals and didn't want to shoot them, but wanted to go with his friends who would make fun of him if he told them the truth. I said there is only thing you can do is shoot blanks.

Four guys were in the country target shooting. After the three of them had their turn they all stood near the target. I thought that was dangerous. They said it was the safest place to be because he misses the target by a mile.

Even on a trip hunters have a difficult time relaxing. They go on a river trip and want to shoot the rapids.

If a hunter has trouble he calls in a trouble shooter.

Sometimes all basketball players talk is dribble.

When you lose a well fought game you should think of the positive side of losing. Think how happy you made the other team feel.

The last two runners in a race are far behind. The one turned to the other and said we have a lot of catching up to do.

A basketball player who played center didn't play well. We can say he was off center.

The manager told the baseball player to keep his eye on the ball and quit worrying about the girls.

When a boy dreams about being a basketball star these are called "Hoop dreams."

When a baseball player doesn't know what to say he is spitless. When he's upset you don't want to be within spitting distance.

A baseball player says he travels all over but never forgets his home base. He was going over figures with his accountant to see if he could afford something. He says yes the figures are in the ballpark. The best compliment you can give him is to say he has his eye on the ball.

A baseball player got a good hit and made it past first and ran to second, but there was no second base nor was there a third base. The player before him stole second and third base.

 A lot of us are like baseball players, if we get too many strikes against us we are out of the game.

They asked the baseball player why he thought he was walked twice during the game. He said he was such a good hitter they didn't dare let him hit the ball.

Baseball is catching on all over the world. The manager said when he asked for a heavy hitter, he didn't mean an overweight player.

Baseball players can be so boring. They are always talking about their big hit and going over and over it.

A runner said he would go the distance for his girlfriend.

A runner tried to pass another runner. The first runner put his hand out and said "This is a no passing zone." Before the race the one runner talked to the other runners about how they always bunch up in front. He said it would be better if they stayed behind him. A runner said he just caught his second wind and would have won the race if the time hadn't run out.

A boxer's famous punch line "I am going to get you, you sucker".

A hunter is upset. He feels like his life has been spent.
He is down to his last shot. His aim is off.
He feels he has been the unfair target of others.
He doesn't even feel like game anymore.

Two guys were hunting. One shot an elk. The other guy asked if he thought he had helped. The other one said sure. Well than can I have the bragging rights.

A hunter who likes to shoot too much is said to be trigger happy.

Three guys went hunting. I asked one if they had a good time. He said no, Joe called all the shots.

A golfer can be too busy when he has too many irons in the fire.

Track coach to his runners. Now let's run through this again.

At one game all the members of a team struck out. I wondered what was up. Later I found out that they were on strike.

A bowler when he is on top of the game is bowled over.
He sees problems like pins that need to be knocked over.
He has the ball to do it.
He aims to strike them down.
Sometimes he doesn't get them and there is a spare, but he just keeps on trying.
When he is down you could say he is in the gutter.

A former basketball player had not played in a couple of years. He felt like he was out of the loop.

While playing golf one golfer was going to help another one with his swing. The third golfer said leave him alone. There are different strokes for different folks.

A boxer used to lay carpet. He tells his opponent that he is going to lay him out like a rug.

A boxer said he has to do a few rounds before he is warmed up but than he is hot.

A fighter always has a chance. He has a fighting chance.

A wrestler complained to the trainer after practice that he felt a pain on his chest and asked what he should do. The trainer said tell the other guy to get off your chest.

The news in a fighter's magazine is jaw breaking.

A baseball player is discouraged. He says all he wants to do is run home. Baseball players not only need to cover their bases, but they need to keep in touch with their bases.
The word all baseball players want to hear "Your safe."

If a cowboy was playing football he would say cut them off at the pass.

Two young black guys were playing basketball when two young white guys came over and challenged them to a game. After awhile one of the guys said we really should play shirts against skins so we know who is on what team.

Ask a baseball player why he didn't go home. He says he was called out.

Sometimes when talking to a runner they don't get it. You have to run that by them again.

Did you ever figure out why basketball players are called jocks? I can only think it must be for the jock straps they wear.

A skier always said "Let's hit the slopes." When he works out he says "Let's hit the machines."

Two guys were playing tennis. The one who lost said his game was a little off today. His friend said your game has never been on.

Runner says I am now going to give you the rundown on the today's events.

A football player said there is no problem too big that he can't tackle it.

An ex baseball player is no longer interested in baseball. He doesn't even care who is on first.

A baseball player said home plate is always where his home is.
When someone tries to tell him advice that he doesn't like he tells them they are way off base.

A basketball player says to two other players, "I bet you can't get the jump on me."

Why do we always want to play the winner? It would be easier to play the loser.

A baseball player retired claiming he was all played out.

A fighter said he is always accused of starting the fight.

They were playing a neighborhood game of football. When asking one boy what the score was, he said was 35 to 3 their favor. But he said nobody was keeping score.

A baseball player is the only one who admits to running around.

A runner is running in place. He said when he was little and wanted to run off his mother would tell him not to run off, so he learned to run in place. Also this can be found up North when it is cold and you want to stay warm.

The coach kind of likes me. He said if I play ball with him he will give me some free throws.

When I run, I like to run against someone and not the clock.

The baseball player chewed tobacco. He had a difficult time saying what he meant and would sometimes stutter. One impatient guy told him to just spit it out. You may not want to say that to a chewer.

A baseball player is upset with another player from another team. He hates it when someone beats him at his own game.

We are told to be like people who are in sports. People will say to us "Be a good sport."

You don't want to get all choked up when it is your turn to bat.

Teachers/Students

A teacher in a seventh period class asked the one boy why he never raised his hand. He said by this time of the day his body odor was pretty bad.

A boy wrote back from a prep school that the school was full of vampires. They are even encouraging us to give our blood in a fake blood drive.

What all teachers want to do for you. Teach you a lesson.

A student was called into the principal's office. The student asked what was wrong. It was an open book test and he only had one book. The problem was it was the answer book.

The teachers think a male teacher is in love with the cleaning lady. His room is always so messy it takes the cleaning lady twice as long to clean his room.

When a math teacher threatens someone, she says your days are numbered.

When she is feeling defeated she feels like she is outnumbered.

A math student said he couldn't do his math because someone had borrowed his calculator and hadn't returned it.

What college students don't want to run out of, is excuses.

An algebra teacher said the unknown in his life is the X factor. He never knows what his X is going to do.

A student doesn't like his grade. He asks the teacher if she can upgrade it.

When angry the math teacher says count to ten.

An English teacher said her butcher husband was butchering the English language.

Why do student have to take Algebra I? So later they make them take Algebra II.

The students got their papers back and they had all done badly. One student asked the teacher if he couldn't just count this a trial run.

A student to the math teacher who had told them they were going to be learning long division. He said "You know I can't do that I have a short attention span."

An elementary teacher said she would put red marks on their papers when the answers were wrong. One student got his paper back with lots of red checks. He told the teacher "You know you can go to jail for writing bad checks"

History teacher to student says I know we have had this conversation before, but you really have to do better on your work. The student says "I know it is sort of like history repeating itself."

When a man called a math teacher and asked her for a date she said boy do you have the wrong number.

A mother visited her son in an elementary classroom. She noticed he sat in front by the teacher. She asked if that was so the teacher could keep an eye on him. He said no the teacher told him that was because he was the head of the class.

When the students in a teacher's room do good she says it is a class act.

A teacher tells noisy classroom they have the right to remain silent.

A health teacher threatened a student by saying, "You will do it, if you know what is good for your health."

My teacher doesn't trust me or think I know anything. He is always quizzing me.

I told my history teacher that what is in the past should remain in the past. I don't want anyone bringing up my past. And if I have trouble remembering my Mother and girlfriend's birthday I sure am not going to be able to remember all these dates from way back.

It is okay to do some cutting up in biology class.

An English teacher said in my class we don't use abbreviations, we use whole language.

When you come to the English class you are told to watch your language.

The math teacher's boyfriend said he also worked with numbers. He was a gambler.

The direction you don't want your grades to go is South.

A student complains to the teacher. "You mean there is a right and wrong answers. You are taking all the fun out of guessing."

A student says the math teacher is so unfair. You don't even get any credit for being close.

The English teacher knew he was the man for her when they first met and she found out that he was hooked on phonics.

After receiving his grade a student told the teacher that he felt degraded.

A student put his head down on the desk. The teacher asked what was wrong. He said he had just been learning to much in his head and it gave him a headache.

When the teacher wants the student's attention she says "heads up."

A science teacher who tries something different is said to out of his element.

A student in a math class is so demanding. When his numbers don't add up right he demands a recount.

Students who are deep thinkers go to the School of Thought. Now of course some go to a different School of Thought.

A science teacher said that some of the student's reports read like science fiction.

Some college students are getting a room ready for a banquet. There guys were working, but one was just holding his girlfriend. They asked him to help, but he said "Can't you see I have my hands full?"

A math teacher with a poor self-image doesn't count himself.
The grade school teacher said the task was so easy it was elementary.

The assignment in class was to write a short story. All of them did, but one student. When asked why he didn't write one he said he suffered from a writer's block.

A drama teacher was having trouble with a student who couldn't learn his lines. Finally she gave up and gave him one liners.

Your professor is brilliant. He talks over the heads of everybody. Nobody understands anything he says. A sure sign of brilliance on the college campus.

A teacher says that if he had put this box on the test most of the students would have checked it. The box says "I don't know."

A teacher handing back the students work told them to go over their mistakes and find some time to correct them. One student said my Dad said we shouldn't focus too much on our mistakes.

An English teacher said it isn't a good idea to have the seniors write about what they did last summer. Some how it creeps them out.

A student yells "I got it right." Teacher well there is always a first time for anything.

A math teacher says when you date someone always look for their pluses and minuses.

The teacher's room is so noisy. When she calls for a minute of silence that is all she gets.

A suspicious math teacher always wants to know what is their angle. She tells her boyfriend not to be a square.

A reading teacher got a job in the police department. She worked in the evidence room. Her job was to proof read.

The math teacher is so unfair. He has so many problems and when we get to class he gives them to us and expects us to solve them for him. Another student said since he has math classes his problems have been multiplying. A third student asked if there was a leader in the division.

If a math teacher fought a battle they would divide and conquer.

Around the end of the semester the teachers get so testy. A student said he was all tested out.

A student was asked by the teacher what he got out of a long boring book they were assigned to read. He said lots of sleep.

A student having trouble in math said his count was off.

A teacher asked a student what he thought about a certain idea. He said he liked to keep his ideas to himself.

Many a chaperone has gone nuts when riding a bus while the students were singing 99 bottles of beer on the wall.

When a student is asked if he knows the answer. He answers "yes." He says I like to keep my answers short.

A student in a geography class told his teacher that he had reached his plateau. He wanted to go back to the plains. He just couldn't go around another mountain with his teacher. He had reached his peak.

A history teacher asked the student what was wrong because he had done so poorly on his last few tests. The student said it would help if you sat me by some smart people.

A math teacher asks the student how he could flunk the last five math tests. The student replied that he was on a losing streak.

The theater teacher said he has to much drama in his life.

His son is always acting up.

His daughter thinks she is a star and wants to be the center of the stage.

His wife is tired of her supporting role and wants more.

He tries to direct them to their position and tells them what their lines are.

The roles they are playing are not the ones he designed.

He said there can only be one starting role in the family and it is him.

They kept trying to upstage him.

He may have to pull the curtain on his family.

A father says his daughter is so smart she doesn't even bring an eraser to school.

The student got his paper back from the English teacher with so many marks on it. He asked why. She said earlier she had heard him say "Mark my words."

A math teacher said she has finally meet her equal. When she married him she now feels like a whole number.

All the students on different days brought apple for the teacher. One apple was rotten. You know what they say "There is always one bad apple in the bunch."

A teacher gave a low grade to a student on his paper saying he didn't put much effort into it. He told his friend that the teacher didn't know what she was talking about. "It isn't easy to find the topic and paper on the internet, download it and than recopy it."

Math teachers like the square dance.

Boulder College is located high in the Rockies. They say they have higher learning there.

At middle school you don't want the surprise visitor to be your mother.

Teacher to student says she didn't understand his paper at all. He said thats okay I am often misunderstood.

When a math teachers time on earth is up, we say his number was called.

The professor was so brilliant he decided to donate his brain to science. Imagine the disappointment when a few days later he got a letter of rejection.

The algebra teacher keeps his papers in the X file.

A college student badly needed money for school. His rich uncle was sending him a blank check. When he got the check he showed it to his roommate. His roommate said it might have helped if his Uncle had signed it.

He had been at college at least six years. Finally they heard that their nephew was getting his bar exam. Excited they drove to Dallas to celebrate with him. His parents drove them to a local bar where he was the bartender.

Teacher tells student Stevie Wonder is not one of the seven wonders of the world.

Student to teacher I know I made lots of mistakes. My Dad says we learn from our mistakes. It sure looks like I have been learning a lot lately.

Math teacher's main girlfriend is a prime number.

Student who seldom does good got an A on his test. The teacher said to him "See all your studying and hard work paid off." He thinks and it didn't hurt that I sat behind Carol Ann either.

Never ask a math teach if they have a problem.

The special education math teacher gave everyone a number in class. One student was not doing well and felt down. The teacher told him that he was a special number and that really helped him to feel better.

English teacher to former boyfriend. "You are so past tense."

Trying to date a popular first grade teacher isn't easy. A man found that his name was towards the end of the alphabet on her list.

A history teacher to student tells him he may be right about some things, but having corrected his history paper she can say he is not right about too many things.

A college student says he doesn't like it that everyone is talking about his weight. They call him the big man on campus.

A college athlete twisted his ankle. The doctor wrapped it up and said he would have to stay off it for a couple of days and use crutches. He called the coach and said he couldn't make it to basketball practice. The coach said what lame excuse do you have now?

It is good having the debate coach also be your English teacher. When you disagree with her she says it is open to debate.
A teacher was talking on and on. Finally he said forget that last thing I said. A student to another student "You got to be kidding I don't remember anything he said."

A principal says to the math teachers that they need to quit looking for that perfect number.

I asked a student how he did on the test. He said little did I know.

The math teacher said she always felt safe. There is safety in numbers.

A math teacher that is a little heavy we say she is well rounded.

It isn't easy to be in love with an English teacher. The man would write her love letters, and she would send them back corrected.
A history teacher said she wasn't sure about their relationship because they had a past history together and it wasn't good.
The math teach would treat her husband like he didn't count.
The science teacher thought of their relationship like an experiment that might blow up anytime.
The reading teacher was the best. She said marry me I can read the small print.

When a student's paper came back from the English teacher it was all marked in red. He said it looks like I stand corrected.

A college student frustrated on an exam says he wishes he could demand some answers.

A teacher gave everyone the same problem and the students were to write a plan on how to tackle it. All of them did but one student. He said he didn't want to make a plan that would upset the plans of others.

It can be difficult having a parent who is a teacher.
The boy went to his Mother a math teacher with a problem.
She said you have to learn to solve your own problem.
Another boy complained that when he would say things wrong his mother who was an English teacher would always tell him to say it again and use correct grammar.
Another boy complained that his mother a health teacher always gave him healthy snacks and for twelve years of school no other student would trade lunches with him. He would have loved a candy bar.
Another boy his father is a history teacher and when things happen he always brings up my past history. He says he doesn't want history repeating itself.
The last boy said I had it worse my father was a p.e. teacher. He would take us down the road drop us off and drive a mile further on. He would than time us to see how long it took us to get back to the car.

You have a know it all attitude. You think you are right about everything and you don't like other peoples views. I think you will fit right in with our staff at the university.

A student was sleeping in his afternoon class. He explained to the teacher he had been to Spain in the summer and had gotten used to taking a siesta.

A stress test given in school is when you have to take a test that you are not prepared for.

The math teacher was late for the staff meeting because she had worked to catch up on all her problems.

There is a school of deep thought. You make a decision and than are asked if you thought it through.

The professor hands back the tests. He says the grades were not very good. He says it is partly my fault when before the test I told you to clear your minds. I am afraid many of you went too far in clearing your minds.

A professor hands back the tests. He says I know many of you guessed at the answers. But he says this is a University and at least you need to make an educated guesses.

The Dean of the College is talking to a professor. He tells him he has to do something to make his class more interesting. What I have observed you could be teaching a sleep study class.

A student goes to a class in astronomy. One student asks where are all the beautiful girls. They said they would be studying some heavenly bodies in this class.

Sometimes in life we go around and around to the same problem. The math teacher says that is going full circle.

The elementary teacher told another teacher that what she learned from her third grade class was lots of patience.

Working Out

A guy hugged his right leg a little more than his left leg. Later his left leg started to limp. He said that leg would do anything for attention.

A man couldn't remember which locker he put his clothes. He needed to find them so he could have closure.

A man around the club was blowing a whistle on different people. He said he always wanted to be a whistle blower. I said well some people might get a kick out of it, or you might get a kick out of it.

Two guys were both hanging on a bar. Now that is what I call hanging out together.

An older man said he swims 60 laps every day. I found out later that he did it in the hot tub.

A guy rolls his head from side to side. This is called a head roll.

There were a group of runners at the gym. They had sprint written on their shirts.

A man was lifting weights with his eyes closed. He was bragging that he could do it with his eyes closed.

On the stationary bike a guy lifted his hands in the air and said "Look no hands."

I asked the guy why he wore a coat when he worked out. He said he liked to get warmed up before he worked out.
To tell if you are working out hard all you need to do is to smell under your arm.

A guy was in the sauna. When asked why he wasn't working out he said he told his friends he was going to sweat this one out.

When a man works out and builds lots of muscles, and than quits working out. It is goodbye muscles and hello fat.

There is a new workout program for people in their jobs. The boss doesn't want anyone to say the workers aren't fit for the job.

A new workout place is called "The House of Pain." You know the saying "No pain no gain." If you don't feel the pain when you workout you definitely will when you pay the bill.

In this workout you swing from side to side. It is a workout for swingers.

I don't lift the heavy weights anymore. I just can't afford to buy new shirts.

Backward wave is when you walk forward, but wave with your hands behind you at the people in back of you. It is great they will not know if you are smiling or crying when you leave.

A man in the dressing room had his shirt off and was holding a hair dryer. I asked what he was going to do with the hair dryer. He said he was going to blow his hair dry. I said you are bald. He said the hair on my chest.

The sign at the gym said "If something isn't working report it to the front desk."

This guy was just standing around so I told him I had to report him to the front desk.

A new trainer was hired at the gym. He was on probation at first. They said they were going to watch him and see how he worked out.
A new workout at the gym. A guy is lying down and when he tries to get up different ones knock him down, but he still works to get up. This workout is called "You can't keep a good man down."

There is a new workout for seniors. They bring their mats. Halfway through the workout they all take naps.

Do the mirror workout. You do whatever the other person facing you does. It helps to have an older guy and a younger guy doing this. One can see what he will look like down the road and the other can see what he would like to look like.

A trainer in need of a hug tells girls that it is national hug a trainer day.

I asked a man who was working out if he needs help. He said no he could screw things up by himself. I said but that is not the American way. You get someone to help you and than if it doesn't work out you blame him and if it does you claim the credit.

A new workout is when you lie very still and play dead. During this time you don't hear your wife or boss. This is a must for many husbands, although for most of them it comes naturally.

An older man at the gym came out with his swimming suit on and a towel around him. He went to the front desk and told them his key was stuck in the lock where his clothes were. A worker came to cut the lock. After he cut the lock the worker told the man to look inside and see if that was his stuff. The man did and said I am afraid this isn't my locker. I think my locker might be the one on the other side.

I told the trainers to send the new workout people with me and I would show them a hard workout. We will walk around the gym and I will point out people who are working hard.

A new workout. The trainer yells everyone down with me. Everyone gets down with him. After a minute he says okay now all take a stand with me and everyone stands up. This will help you fit into any group.

When working out don't put your hands down, but put them up. Than you can receive a hand out or a hand up.

A man was holding a big weight up to his chest. When I talked to him he put it down. He said he was glad to get it off his chest.

When you raise your hands and than try to reach your toes that is called the workout of gratefulness. You are saying to your boss you are the greatest thank you for saving my job.

A new workout is called doing the wave. You put both hands up and wave the top of them and say "bye-bye." Great for when you want someone to leave.

A girl had her arms wife open. I asked why so wide. She said she was going to catch a big ball.

One man who hates working out calls the tread mill the dread mill.

I feel like I am covering the same ground over and over again and not getting anywhere. It seems hopeless. I am on the treadmill.

A man was putting a lot of weight on a machine. I said to him you are sure putting on a lot of weight. He said don't get personal.

A man was just working out his one arm. He said he was the boss of company and sometimes he had to use strong arm tactics with the workers.

When you rub your back or your behind against a wall. It is a way of working out and getting rid of an itch.

An older man was in the dressing room half dressed. He said he couldn't remember if he was coming or going.

At the one club there are so many young guys. The showers have only cold water. The young guys are told to take a cold shower.

Some guys were laying down and flapping their hands. They heard because of the cruelty to animals in using seals at Sea World, they are looking to replace the seals with people. Most of them still have to work on their bark.

A guy came to work out wearing sunglasses. Two girls were fanning him. He said they were his fan club.

Work Situations

A anager after watching two workers for a few weeks called them into his office. He said "I would have to say that the way you two work is definitely unskilled".

Four men were carrying boxes. The first three had regular boxes, but the fourth man could hardy carry his box. He said he was left with the heavy lifting.

Firefighters were fighting a grass fire. Tom yelled to the captain that Ted was on fire. The caption yelled back I know Ted has always been one of the best workers.

A dairy farmer said he is not going to cow down to anyone.
He also said he doesn't run after the herd.
He said cows with five stomachs can stomach most anything.
He said he was the one who came up with the saying when the kids spilled the milk. "Don't cry over spilled milk there is plenty more".
He is also the one who said he works at the tail end of the cow.

A secretary had three bosses. One always had ideas that the others didn't think we very good. He found out what the secretary was doing with his ideas. He said "I don't appreciate you filing my ideas under stupid."

The boss was telling a worker about what he thought was dead wrong. The worker said to leave him alone. He said he knew what he was doing. The boss said if you do you are the only one around here who does.

A plumber said he had lots of ideas but they never made it out of the bowl before they were tanked.

Upset photographer said he was getting a fuzzy picture.

A guy said his job was to get material to where it needed to be going. He was accused of being too materialistic.

A seamstress says sometimes her life is like a zipper. She can't get it up or down.

They had to let a worker go at Mrs. Field's Cookies. They caught her with her hand in the cookie jar.

An operator is rather possessive. She doesn't like anyone operating in her area code. She said that other operators aren't operating at full capacity. After years of being an operator she is all rung out. She says she still hears a ringing in her ears.

When a butcher is upset he feels chopped up.

A railroad engineer was having conflict with another engineer. He was always trying to get him off track.

A man went to work for a dog food company. The boss was always barking orders at everyone and it made him nervous. HIs co-worker said not to worry that his bark was worse than his bite.

A worker was always fishing for more information about every situation so she could gossip about it. Finally one worker took care of it. He told her she couldn't fish without a license.

A sign at the grocery store says fresh fruit and vegetables. Underneath that it says that their stockers are so fresh that when your done shopping you are going to feel like slapping them.

The company was in the red. Things didn't look good and everyone would probably lose their jobs. We found the worker with the richest Uncle who was interested in power and prestige and for $50,000 made him a partner.

There was a problem at a packing company. They were told to pack it up and move.
.

A manager told his boss that Jack had walked off the job. The boss not sure who Jack was had the manager show him his picture on the wall. The boss said yes I have seen Jack around here, but I don't think I have ever seen him working.

Worker complaining," I don't like it. He is always telling me what to do and than complains that I don't do it right. He looks over my shoulder when I am working". The other worker says well he is the boss.

There was a business meeting. One man was late getting to it. One of the other men called him and asked what was holding him up. He thought for awhile and than said his belt.

A mechanic was working on my car. He told me he worked in a zoo before. He said they tried to make a monkey out of me. Could you hand me that monkey wrench? I forgot to eat he asked if I could reach the top shelf. He said he kept a bunch of bananas there.. I handed him one. He hates it when his boss calls him a grease monkey.

Who said "Don't give me the slip?" A worker about to receive a pink slip from his boss. A number of workers were let go from the company. When they asked why they were told that it was because of the season. It is the dry season when their is little business.

The only problem about testing the mattresses is that they are so comfortable you won't want to get up.

The manager was going over the directions for a project and was about to tell the workers the directions for the third time. One worker said "You don't need to tell us again were not dumb," Another worker said "Speak for yourself we need the directions again".

Boss says he doesn't have to tell his workers to slow down. Boss said I was going to give some of you time off, but after observing you I believe many of you have been taking time off.

I was good at ballet. Earlier I had a job with a very crabby boss where I always had to be on my toes and learn to dance around his questions.

I felt my boss was using me and not being fair. My coworkers said I needed to stand up to him and confront him. My husband said the same thing. So the next day I decided to take a stand and confront him. I marched right into his office and he said "Hi Rhonda, have a seat." I sat.

I was minding my own business. I was daydreaming about what I would like to be doing. I was laid back with my feet on the desk and almost asleep. Then the boss calls me and asks if that report is done yet. Those demanding bosses.

It is hard to be known as a joker. When he turned in his report to the boss, the boss read it and asked if it was another one of his jokes.

The reporters were going to interview the famous clock maker from Switzerland. We are gong to find out what makes him tick. He said we must be on time. We have to watch what we ask. We must hurry for time is running out. Hopefully we hear a timeless message today.

A reporter at a campaign headquarters said he was searching for the truth about a story. A worker said you won't find it here.

Boss hears manager on phone talking. The manager says sure come on over there is nothing going on here.

Boss to worker I am giving you a few days off. You make so many mistakes that we are all losing time helping you correct your mistakes.

A ranger said he is on the lookout for another job.

They let a lady at the cookie plant go. She had a good attitude about it. She said that's the way the cookie crumbles.

A man who is the manager at an ice cream store says one employee doesn't give a lick about his work.

Laughter that Will Lift Your Spirits

When I got promoted to a higher position in the company I felt elevated.

A laundry worker quit her job. Her boss said you are going to be hard pressed to find another job.

The one salesman hired was a small person. His manager trying to give him confidence said don't sell yourself short.

Not knowing what to say to a dissatisfied customer, the body shop foreman finally says "What's a body to say?"

There is a lot of foot action going on at the shoe store. Also there is tension. You never know when the other shoe is going to drop.

A head of a company was talking to another head of a different company over lunch. He said whatever you do don't have an assertive training class. He said they had one and the trainer taught everyone to learn to say no. Now nobody will stay after work or volunteer for anything.

I asked the armed car driver if he had any change. Boy did he get upset. Some people are just too touchy.

Fired employees in the grocery store get sacked.

The plumber said he couldn't come to work because he was all plugged up.

At a meeting the workers were discussing ideas about what to do with a problem. One worker said he had run out of ideas. A co-worker said you didn't have to run far.

When a computer nerd is told something he doesn't want to hear, he says "It doesn't compute."

A shoe store salesman lost his footing and was demoted. The manager said there was too much flip flopping going on.

It is not a good thing when the director tells the actors he doesn't want to see a repeat performance.

We went to a furniture store. A man was standing around. I asked if he worked here. He said no he just spends his time here.

It is easy to sell to a vampire. A vacuum cleaner salesman would give his talk and the vampier would say "I will bite".

A female worker complaining to another worker about the rough day she had. The other worker asked when did it start? She said when she got out of bed and looked in the mirror and than weighed herself.

A worker noticed that Sharon doesn't seem as sharp as she used to be. A coworker said that was because she had been scared out of her wits earlier.

The postman encouraged me to address every situation as different. The postman likes to talk in codes. He said when they get a letter with the heading "Dearly departed" it always goes in with the dead letters.

Some thought he was witty at work while others thought he was a dimwit.

An electrician said we have to treat people different because they are wired different.

Bosses and mystery club members are part of the Who club. They both want to know Who did it.

At most jobs nobody works that hard to have labor pains.

These people pave our way.
They help us over the bumps in the road.
They help us to get through the rocky roads.
Today let us salute the road workers.

A miner wanted to work with gold and silver, but couldn't find any so he decided to become a dentist so he could work with gold and silver.

Sanitation workers can be in the know. They know what goes on in the alley and who is dumping what. These worker hate it when people trash their name. When they hear the same garbage day after day, it is recycled garbage. One sanitation worker quit his job. He said you can only take so much garbage.

A man at a cemetery digs the graves. I asked him if he always did that. He said no he used to be a ditch digger. People would ask him if he wanted to be a ditch digger all his life, so he became a grave digger.

A bartender told a customer he was keeping tabs on him.

A lab worker said a coworker ratted him out.

A worker at the car wash lost his job. They said he was washed up.

A painter is confused when she starts to mix up the colors.

Boss says of his employees I don't know about idle hands here, but we definitely have idle minds.

A man at work is the target of unfair gossip. He said he is not going to take it standing still. He has now become a moving target.

A trucker says he can be loads of fun. He also says you don't know what is down the road. One time he took a turn for the worse. When he gets old we say he has to many miles on him and he is over the hill.

A chicken farmer said he has had to scratch out a living. And his pay was chicken feed.

Mold was discovered in the school. The janitor said "holy moldy".

A stockbroker said he didn't make much money. There were lots of insider traders, but he was an outsider.

A former conductor on a train now heads a company. After a meeting he asks his coworkers if they are all on board with him.

At a plant when the bell rang it was lunch time. One guy was noticed taking several lunch breaks. When the manager asked him about it, he said he kept hearing bells in his head.

A carpenter had a young man helping him. They had a tape measure and the young man pulled it down to what they were measuring. The carpenter yelled at the young man and asked him how many feet he had. He said two.

Newspaper editor tells another man that he has issues with him.

Newspaper editor tells writer to change his heading from "War declared." It is after all only a price war.

At a conference an annoying guy kept following his coworker around. They found a wishing well. They both made wishes. The annoying guy asked his coworker if he thought his wish would come true. He answered probably not being you are still here.

The highway department is trying to elevate their positions. They even have a "Road Scholar" program. It helps pave the way for students to be successful.

A news team is sent out to interview the famous Cat woman. She has a house full of cats. A reporter says let's hope she opens the door so we can have a word with her. The door opens the reporter quickly asks her if she has anything to say. She says "Me ow" and slams the door. The reporter says to the other reporter "Did you see her claws?" Well there you have it folks, but she is still under investigation. It has been reported that there is a cat burglar in the neighborhood.

Boss says "This is the last time I am saying this." One employee to another says he is glad. He is so tired of hearing the boss say the same thing over and over again.

The boss had asked who was available to work overtime. Kip asks if he can work overtime. The boss said I would rather see you working during your regular time.

A postal worker said things go so fast some things just zip right past him.

Boss talking to Luke in a group says I know Luke you have some ideas, but right now we are looking for good ideas.

Our team tried to come up with a good plan. We put our heads together. All we came up with was a headache.

Four guys were called into the office. They were told by the boss to clean out their desks. The one an optimist said "Great we are going to get new desks."

At the company when they say there is an overflow they are talking about an overflowing toilet.

A manager who has an office on the 10th floor says to some new workers. Remember I started out on the ground floor once.

At the company picnic they always had games and contests. The one guy always ran the stopwatch. He was a natural being he watched the clock all day.

A shirt says "We got the Power." Of course I know they work at the power company.

A moving truck is hauling the fireman's things. You could say the firemen are on the move..

Man in military wanted to quit. His mother wrote "Soldier on."

Sign in a sport store selling basketballs. "More for your bounce here."

The workers work in cubicles. Several complained about the one worker they said he snored so loud it prevented the rest of them from getting any sleep.

Boss to employee if you want a paid vacation you have to do some work first.

At our company every time there is work to do we have a lot of MIA missing in action.

A rug salesman said he was feeling very discouraged. Things were just not running good for him. He said was like the rug was being pulled out from beneath him.

A man in an office building started to light a cigarette. His coworker said he needed to take it outside. He fell to his death. He worked on the twelfth floor.

Editor looking over the writer's writing says it looks like we are thinking along the same lines.

Substitute at information desk was not working out too well. When asked where something was he would say "I don't know or beats me."

The worker they really liked at the information desk knows what is going on in the stores and all the latest gossip about the workers.

A guy made a very good point, but his competitive co-worker called his point a power point. So much competition at work.

The latest fad in insurance buying is the no fault insurance. Two cars just ran into each other at an intersection, but is just happens, and it's nobody's fault. Don't you love it when nobody gets the blame?

A worker at a job where they are expected to come up with lots of ideas said he had few, but he did have lots of dreams. I asked why. He said that's what happens when you sleep on the job.

After twenty years the company with the bright ideas was closing. If things were ideal they could remain open, but unfortunately they just ran out of ideas.

When I checked out of the grocery store, the clerk said I saved eleven dollars, but wasted twenty on junk food and things I didn't need.

A customer was complaining to the travel agent about all the problems they had on their trip. He looked at their sign which said "Dream Vacation." He said our vacation was a nightmare. Well the travel agent said nightmares can be a part of dreams.

He worked for the clockmaker but didn't like it. He said it was too much like clockwork and at the last job he got tired of the clock. He watched it pretty much all day. He said he was clocking out and leaving.

The manager of the different departments always had plenty of ideas but when they brought them to the boss at their monthly meeting the ideas were DOA dead on arrival.

The construction foreman says when he hires new workers he likes them to start in the basement and work their way up to the top.

A parking attendant got fired. They said he was doing a bang up job.

The lady politician has her makeup and lipstick smeared. The rumor is that she is running a smear campaign.

A carpenter that drinks too much we say he is hammered.

The man that works at the funeral home looked at the urns of those that were cremated and said to his boss those are the remains of the day.

A pilot said his job is so routine that sometimes he is on automatic pilot. He does have a carefree attitude. You could say he is flying high.

A sign at an information booth says "Boy have I got information for you!